The Therapist in Therapy

The Therapist in Therapy

JAMIE MASEROW

First published by The Kind Press in 2025
thekindpress.com

Text copyright © Jamie Maserow, 2025
All rights reserved.
No part of this publication may be reproduced without prior written permission from the publisher.

We at The Kind Press acknowledge that Aboriginal and Torres Strait Islander peoples are the Traditional Custodians and the first storytellers of the lands on which we live and work; and we pay our respects to Elders past and present.

A catalogue record for this book is available from the National Library of Australia.

ISBN: 9781763508378 (paperback)

DISCLAIMER

The diagnosis and treatment of mental illness requires a trained, qualified mental health practitioner. Information contained in this book is intended to provide readers with personal experiences and insights only and should not be used as a substitute for professional diagnosis and/or treatment of any mental illness. Some names, locations and identifying characteristics of individuals in this book have been changed to protect the privacy of those depicted.

Dedicated –
to making the world a better place.

Contents

FOREWORD by Moshe Lang ix

CHAPTER	1	My First Steps	1
CHAPTER	2	The Blessing and the Curse of Covid	13
CHAPTER	3	Anxiety	23
CHAPTER	4	From Small Talk to Medium Talk	35
CHAPTER	5	Communication	43
CHAPTER	6	Bringing a Family Member to Therapy	53
CHAPTER	7	Thick Skin	61
CHAPTER	8	My Covid Story	71
CHAPTER	9	The L Word	83
CHAPTER	10	Becoming a Psychologist	91
CHAPTER	11	Welcome to the Jungle	103
CHAPTER	12	Psychology With Moshe	111
CHAPTER	13	Self Care	123
CHAPTER	14	Hour 44	137
CHAPTER	15	Friends	149
CHAPTER	16	Wedding Season	161
CHAPTER	17	Hour 45	169
CHAPTER	18	Lessons From Covid	183
CHAPTER	19	Story Time	197
CHAPTER	20	Baptism by Fire	207
CHAPTER	21	My Intention	221
CHAPTER	22	Becoming More Myself	237

AFTERWORD In Conversation with Moshe *255*
References *260*
About the author *262*

Foreword

by Moshe Lang

I have written on and off for an untold number of years about my work with different people. I never think of anybody as a 'client' or a 'patient' – they are the person who comes to see me and we talk. I have always been very keen to encourage people who have been on the other side of the coffee table to tell their story about our work from their perspective. I imagined we would do it together, one way or another, but the way it developed with Jamie – and I am convinced the process was right – is that she was better off writing this book on her own. Because the key thing for writers is to find their own voice, and sometimes even something like a limited vocabulary is a big advantage. If you have a limited vocabulary, you have to be more creative in expressing what you want with less. There is a beautiful English expression for that – less is more.

What convinced me that Jamie was a writer is that she could get into a flow and write for six hours. It has been a source of joy for her, and at the end of the day I feel privileged to have had the opportunity to play a part in it, to encourage and facilitate it. I am happy not to know anything about what Jamie has written, though I am very curious, I can contain my curiosity. I have done a lot of interactive writing and co-writing, but I am not really a writer.

In our therapy two main things stood out for me, at the beginning and still now, as the issues in Jamie's life – issues that have had consequences with her relationship to men. How I understand it, how Jamie understands it and why it is like that is what we have explored and will continue to do so.

In working with Jamie, I do not wish to have power, and what I wish is to foster a relationship of collaboration and co-operation. What has worked for her in therapy and between the two of us is the matching. What I had to offer is something that she wanted, needed and has taken. It works the other way round, too – matching is a two-way thing. Therapy is no different to other human interactions. For it to be effective, we need to be on the same wavelength, and between Jamie and I there is a mutual flow of understanding and conversation.

I have been a supervisor for psychologists for many years and have found that many of them feel that their patients don't listen to them. In fact, the word 'listen' is complicated in the English language because it has two meanings. I hope that you listen to me in the sense that you hear me. I don't want you to listen to me in the sense of obeying me (which is the other meaning).

If you listen to me, in the sense of following what I am telling you, I feel freer to tell you what I think if I know that you will assess it for yourself and, in the end you'll do what makes sense to you, not to me. The less power therapists seek, the more power they have.

A very well known family therapist, Jay Hayley wrote a book called *The Power Tactics of Jesus Christ*. And I guess I use those tactics on Jamie. I don't seek any power, I don't want to have any power, and I have been happy for her to go the way she chooses to go. I believe that Jamie has made what are good choices for her. Seeing her make these choices is evidence of her feeling more secure, confident and autonomous, which is what I wanted her to do. My job is to make myself redundant, not to make Jamie more dependent.

The way Jamie practised her psychology was not part of my brief, so I never went into it. I didn't see it as relevant to what I was engaged to do. I never understood her approach to psychology, and my world and my thinking is very different. But what I do know is that the way Jamie relates to the people she works with would make her a good psychologist. What has stood out to me, and it is important, is that she is a young woman who likes her work. It gives her a lot of pleasure and joy. And Jamie is not so disconnected from life that she would enjoy it if she wasn't good at it. She enjoys it because the kids want to talk to her and the parents feel happy with her, etc.

Jamie is articulate, intelligent and vivacious – she is full of life. She is also sensitive, and her judgement in choosing a therapist is of course peerless! I thought when I first met her, and I still think, that she has a lot going for her, and she has probably written about it in this book. In everything, the biggest surprise for me is her writing and the joy it has given her.

CHAPTER 1

My First Steps

Moshe Lang. It had to be Moshe Lang, the psychologist who I would go and see, and no one else. His name came to me in the middle of the night, around 3 am, when I knew it was finally not only time but essential for me to speak with someone. As a young psychologist myself, I didn't want to talk to a 'me'. I needed someone with wisdom, knowledge, and experience – someone who I would respect, and who I would want to listen to. I worked in an office filled with exceptionally experienced, kind, caring and intelligent psychologists who fit those criteria exactly. I considered asking one of them to be my psychologist, but realised it was too close to home. I couldn't do therapy in the physical environment where I am a therapist myself. I knew it wouldn't work, and it wouldn't be fair to either of us.

There was a girl who I would see and her family story had several similarities to my own. Initially it was very triggering for me to see her, but I felt that I understood her story more than she will ever know. In one of our sessions, Moshe's name was mentioned, and so he must have been somewhere in the back of my mind.

When I woke up the next morning, I tried to phone Moshe's office three times, with no answer. I Googled him and found he is 'one of Australia's best known family therapists' with more than five decades of experience, and I believed he would *know* my story all too well. Years before I had listened or watched one of his podcasts for emerging psychologists. I tried to call him again on the Tuesday morning and again no one answered the phone. On Wednesdays, I consulted nearby to Moshe's rooms. When I finished work, I decided I would go to the Williams Road Psychotherapy Centre and try to speak to someone. The door was open, so I walked in through the corridor to reception where it was empty. I was so confused.

I noticed that the feel at Williams Road Psychotherapy Centre was very different to the feel of my office. The furniture was old and wooden. It had a serious ambience and was very quiet and tranquil. I described my office as a playground for children's psychology. It was bright and colourful, the rooms were filled with board games, dolls houses and fidget toys and the waiting room was lively and noisy.

I decided to leave a note in reception for Moshe, hoping it would get to him. There was an email address published on his website, but knowing he was close to my grandfather's age I thought a note was the safest method of communication.

In my mind, I know how psychology practices work and never imagined I would be able to see Moshe himself – I thought he would be fully booked and would refer me to another psychologist. I know that because it had happened several times in my office. Clients would call up wanting an assessment for their children with more experienced psychologists and they ended up with me. But I didn't want a me, I wanted Moshe Lang, and for some reason I was lucky enough to get Moshe Lang.

Hi Moshe

I hope you are well. My name is Jamie Maserow and I just popped past to see if I could chat to someone on reception but it is quiet here. I need some help please and I am just wondering (hoping) if you are taking on new clients at the moment ...

I am a psychologist myself and have listened to some of your podcasts before!

Kind regards,

Jamie

That afternoon I received a phone call from Moshe, who was surprised I was a girl. As I signed off the note 'Kind regards, Jamie' he had imagined Jamie being a boy. Moshe told me he had a cancellation the following day, at 2 pm and I truly couldn't believe it. I told him how excited and happy I was and that I would most definitely be there. He told me he liked my *chutzpah* and that in the forty years of consulting, no one had ever left him a note like that before. And I felt better about my upcoming appointment knowing that I had seen the venue and knew what to expect.

Moshe doesn't know this, but when I went to my GP

the following morning, she noticed a freckle on my scalp and was concerned that it may be cancerous. So, in the appointment, I got my Mental Health Care Plan and a referral to a dermatologist, which understandably caused me considerable anxiety. I remember calling my dear mum on the way to Moshe's saying, 'Mum, should I tell Moshe I might have a melanoma or should I discuss my real problems?' I was so anxious, and she said, 'No Jamie, don't be ridiculous, just talk about your real problems – there's no point in worrying about the freckle until we know the outcome.' A lesson she has taught me countless times in my life – most of the things we worry about don't happen. And here we are. Thankfully my freckle was just a freckle, and I have been privileged enough to have spent nearly fifty hours with Moshe Lang as my psychologist – something I will be eternally grateful for.

Moshe's office was upstairs, and I remember being very impressed at the start that before each session he would walk down the stairs and back up to let me into his room. His office was big, and I counted that it had seventeen pieces of art framed on the walls. Knowing Moshe better now, I know each artwork has a story behind it or likely be by a friend of his. The paintings I love the most are the ones with flowers. One is a scribbled artwork that I imagine came from one of his grandchildren or a young child he worked with, but I have never asked him.

Moshe and I sit on old, blue couches opposite each other. In between us there is a coffee table with Moshe's Japanese tea (it's delicious, and he used to give me some each session before COVID), a tissue box, his diary which he writes appointments in and other papers he has either written on or papers that have been printed out for him. Far behind Moshe to the right-hand side is a desk piled with papers that looks like it hasn't been touched in twenty years. It is a mess. I always wondered what all the papers were and why Moshe hadn't cleaned it up. Next to the desk was a bookshelf filled with books and to the left of our couches was a wooden cabinet piled with multiple versions and copies of the three books Moshe published.

Moshe is a small man with no hair. He speaks in a thick Israeli accent, which somehow makes him seem even cleverer to me. He is always the same – very calm when I enter his room, even when I am not. I have never taken note of the way he dresses in detail, but I have noticed he sits very comfortably in his chair. He thinks before he speaks, and most of the time he looks directly at me unless he is really thinking about what to say, when he will look to the left behind me.

Fast forward two and a half years and in a session with Moshe, I asked him if he was writing a book about the benefits of COVID and he looked at me and said, 'Jamie, I am writing five books in my head at the moment, but not unless you want to write them with me.' We laughed it off and continued our session.

Later that night, I went home, reflected, and thought about his comment '… not unless you want to write them with me'. I decided that this would be the most perfect opportunity, and I would write a book with Moshe. I even thought about how his life would be much more routine than mine, how I would most likely need to set a time each week (something I am not good at doing) to write with him and, how fun and honourable it would be to write a book together. I also thought he should write one more book, and COVID would be a very interesting topic from his perspective. I did worry how we could write a book together while he continued to be my therapist and I knew it was probably not possible, but I thought we could discuss it and come to a suitable conclusion.

His mobile number was saved in my phone from our telehealth sessions, and I was tempted to call him every single day following this appointment. I decided, however, that it was a conversation to have face-to-face and it truly tested my patience to wait. When our next appointment arrived, I started rambling on and said, 'Moshe, I don't know how to ask you this…' He laughed and said, 'Try using English.' I suggested my idea about a COVID book, and he answered, 'Jamie, while there have been several benefits of the pandemic, I worry it would be too insensitive to the people who have truly struggled, lost family members and businesses they had built over the years. Imagine if one of your grandparents died from COVID, it would not be a blessing to you.' He also told me he is not a writer but a 'conversationalist and a storyteller', and we had a back-and-forth discussion about the idea.

After some time, he said, 'How about this. You write the book on your own about your experience of being in therapy with me. Many psychologists, including myself, write about how we help clients, but we rarely write about receiving help ourselves. You can record our sessions moving forward, we can discuss your ideas and clarify any questions you have with me in the sessions.' Moshe told me not to worry about publishing it, to write it raw and as real as possible, and if I did ever want to publish it, I could use a pseudonym for him and me, or for me and use his real name. He said I might never publish it, or maybe one day I would show it to my 'daughter'. He specifically said daughter a few times, and not son. *I wonder why?*

It was always on my bucket list to write a book. My plan was to wait until I was older and wiser, but I knew what I wanted to write. I have several journals filled with special quotes that have stood out to me over my life and my travels. Each chapter would begin with one of the quotes and I would then write about that topic. Instead, you will notice that I have sprinkled these quotes throughout this writing. I had previously explained my idea to Moshe, and throughout one session I saw him thinking deeply. He said, 'Jamie, I am distracted by the idea of the book,' as he looked to the left behind me. I got very, very excited when I realised that maybe I didn't have to be 'old' to write my book, that maybe my time to write was now.

Maybe I will publish it and maybe it will just be saved on my laptop for myself and Moshe to look through in our sessions, I thought to myself. Moshe also said that not only would it help me deeply with my own healing process (as he has always encouraged me to write) but it would help me just as much as a practising psychologist.

What you will see, however, is that my book and writing have unfolded in a way I didn't expect. I guess, in the same way, much about life does not unfold the way we expect it to. But it always works out in the end. And for me, although Moshe declined my offer, it was a perfect outcome. I would write my book with his help, guidance and wise words and still be able to see him for my fortnightly sessions.

CHAPTER 2

The Blessing and the Curse of Covid

Early on in therapy, I was chatting with Moshe's receptionist before a session and decided to buy his book *Resilience*. It is a book he and his late wife Tesse wrote about his stories of therapy over the years. This book is one that I never ever wanted to end. I probably read it in a day or two and have since passed it on to several other people to read. Moshe wrote about his clients' stories, and I have always wondered what he would write about me. Maybe I should ask him.

Throughout the pandemic, while I, like everyone else, was up and down, I was mainly up and did not mind lockdowns too much. In fact, there was a lot about lockdown life I thoroughly enjoyed. At certain stages it felt strange to go on walks with my friends as I was so incredibly happy and was thriving when many people around me were understandably lonely, depressed, bored and frustrated. My safe place to discuss this outside my immediate family was with Moshe, where I could tell him everything honestly with no judgement. This led us to having many conversations about some of the 'benefits of COVID' that were not nearly as widely discussed as the 'tragedy' of COVID.

A little later, out of the blue, Moshe sent me a link to a live Zoom talk he did with parents of a local school, in which he had spoken about the blessing and the curse of COVID. This talk was brilliant and there were so many themes that emerged that I thought we needed to hear as a society.

At the start of his talk Moshe talked about how, in being confronted with difficulties and put out of our comfort zones, we as individuals must find skills and abilities, we never imagined we could have. He explained that to give birth you experience pain, crisis and opportunity, and in cultures, stress, anxiety and challenge can lead to growth. I was fortunate enough to grow so much throughout lockdowns, largely due to my work with Moshe. When things felt hard, I said, 'Moshe, this feels uncomfortable – when will it go away?' He explained to me that my discomfort was 'growing pains' and that they would never go away. I like the idea of growing pains, even though they are so annoying at the time. 'I'm sick of growing,' I would say, and he would gently laugh.

> *"The only evidence of life is growth! This is also true in the psychological world. If you are growing, you are alive."*
> —Dr. Wayne W. Dyer, *Your Erroneous Zones*

Another theme of Moshe's talk was how to manage the sense of unpredictability in the chaos of Melbourne stage 3 and 4 lockdowns. We Melbournians, had one of the longest, toughest lockdowns in the world, and it was felt in the energy in the streets, in the children, in the adults and in the elderly. It was dull, scary and tiring, but the fact of the matter is that there was nothing we could do about it. Being in lockdown was not something that we could control, and it was something we all had to face, whether we liked it or not. In his talk, Moshe explicitly said, 'I haven't got a special answer in how to deal with it. You deal with it in the best way you know how.' He went on to explain that life is generally unpredictable, and as humans we need to develop the capacity, resilience, and tolerance to deal with the tension and ambiguity that is part of life. He is right.

'We make plans and G-d laughs,' another lesson my mum taught me. As a young girl I thought I had the most perfect family. I saw the incredible love between my parents. Never did I imagine it would come crashing down the way it did. I never thought my parents would get divorced. I never thought I would spend half of my life living in a different country to my dad. I never thought my dad would have a wife I didn't like, or a girlfriend younger than me. I never thought I would fight with him the way we have. I never thought my mum would get a new husband. I never thought I would be so terrified of dating and being vulnerable. But change is an inevitable part of life, and we need to be able to deal with it when things don't go the way we want them to.

> *"Experience is what you get when you didn't get what you wanted."*
> —Randy Pausch, *The Last Lecture*

During his Zoom talk, an audience member asked Moshe, 'How do we know what we should worry about? We tell ourselves and the parents of our school that we shouldn't sweat the small stuff. Do you agree? How can we be sure we know what the small stuff is, and what should we worry about and leave in the minor annoyance category?'

Moshe answered, 'That is part of being wise, that is what wisdom is, and I haven't got an answer to how to improve your wisdom.'

I loved his honesty and totally agreed – no one can tell you what the small stuff is, and it is, in my opinion, completely different for each individual and circumstance. A large proportion of what I talk about and need the most help with from Moshe (e.g., how to go on a date) would be *small stuff* to other people, whereas to me it is big and hard stuff.

Moshe went on to elaborate his answer and took a stance that is very relevant to psychology in general. He said, 'Sometimes to act on something small is the most important thing. I would say sweat the small stuff. The first step is the most difficult one. It is very important to take the small step and sometimes it is the scariest of them all.' I have said this in our first session to many of my clients: 'Well done, you are so brave – this might be the hardest session because I am a stranger to you, and you are opening up to me and hopefully it will never again be as hard to come here as it was today.' Funnily enough the same applied to my own situation. It was really difficult for me to get to the point, as a 27-year-old (I would say girl, but Moshe would probably say adult or young woman), of realising that I really needed help and psychological support. I had reached the point where not only did I know I had to speak to someone, but I knew I needed to act quickly before I changed my mind about it (hence me literally stalking Moshe).

Another question from the audience was: 'How do you recommend people deal with teenagers who don't want to leave their house? What would you recommend they do?' 'I don't know how to answer that,' Moshe said, laughing. He suggested swapping the children with other families whose parents are upset that their children are always out, and then everyone would be happy. I laughed as I heard this. Moshe explained it would be disrespectful to the children to answer this question as he doesn't know them, and that he doesn't know what is going on in their lives. This reminded me of one of the most helpful pieces of advice I had received from a first psychology mentor. When I was a nervous-wreck psychologist starting out, she said, 'The best piece of advice I can give you is that it is okay not to know the answer. If you are in a session and you don't know the answer, tell the clients that and get back to them later.' Here Moshe was doing exactly that – being honest and vulnerable and not pretending he knew everything, which for a young, early-career psychologist is something that does not come easily.

To the question, 'What advice should you give a teenage daughter who feels so disappointed at the opportunities she is missing?' Moshe answered by explaining the importance of showing empathy, understanding and support to the children on the one hand, 'and on the other hand,' he said, 'sooner or later we all have to grow up. Part of growing up is understanding that your father doesn't always know best… parents don't control the environment, they can't stop COVID or the rain coming… and that part of growing up is learning to deal with life's disappointments.'

As I re-watched his talk and typed up his words verbatim, I felt as if he was speaking directly to me. I believe the reason I came to see Moshe was to grow up, in a sense, to shape my adulthood while learning to deal with the disappointment's life had thrown at me.

I laughed and laughed throughout his talk, as I had known him fairly well by then, and often thought that we reacted the same way to some of the questions. Moshe is very straightforward and cleverly simplifies situations that we make complicated in our heads. When I discussed this idea with Moshe, his response was, 'You say it's clever and I say it is so bloody obvious.'

As I was trying to find his talk in my emails to rewatch it when I wrote this chapter, I found the following feedback I sent him at the time:

> 'Moshe, I thoroughly enjoyed watching this video – thank you for sharing it. The parts I loved most were your very honest answers and respect towards the audience… e.g. the children of the parents' asking questions. I will remember, next time I want to check in with a friend to see how they are, to simply to say, 'How are you?'

CHAPTER 3
Anxiety

A significant part of Moshe's school talk was about anxiety, since many people in Melbourne, and no doubt the rest of the world, had faced more anxiety in the past two COVID years than ever before. From my perspective, the anxiety in some ways came on a collective level as so much was unknown. Would we die from COVID? Did we currently have it without knowing it? Would our jobs be halted? Would we have enough money to pay rent or mortgage? Would schools shut down? And later, would schools ever return? Would travel start again? Would we ever be able to plan a wedding? Around the whole world a significant portion of those two years had been spent in the unknown. No matter how educated, successful or rich you were, everyone was in it together. No one could give us the answers, and no one, not even the greatest psychologists, could take the anxiety away.

Moshe explained that anxiety can be communicated on a subconscious level – anxious people make you anxious too. I now understood why I felt so anxious and uptight after seeing some clients. What he explained is that it is very important to get to know your anxiety, in fact to 'ideally to befriend your anxiety'. I love how he switched the conversation around and explained that anxiety is not necessarily a bad thing. It is a normal human reaction in some circumstances, and furthermore, it may even be a serious problem not to experience anxiety.

Moshe seemed to be recommending that you get to know your anxiety as much as you can – to understand when it is appropriate and helpful and what to do about it. He said that how you understand your anxiety is more significant than the actual anxiety itself. I like this idea and probably need to explore it more with my own clients. Moshe explained to me that part of my understanding of anxiety may also be an aspect of the way psychology is being taught today. 'It is taught as if it is a sub-branch of medicine. Anxiety is seen as a medical condition rather than as an aspect of life that can be seen in both positive and negative ways, and it is usually both. All of life is full of contradiction.'

Moshe continued with an example of a young man who came to see him because, allegedly, he was diagnosed with severe anxiety. He didn't like the psychologist he had been seeing because he always got reduced to his diagnosis. He asked Moshe about his anxiety and why he used the words 'what you call anxiety'. Moshe replied, 'Because anxiety is just one way of looking at it.' He asked the young man to imagine himself as a footballer, and all your life you dreamed that one day you would be so successful and play for whoever your team is. To imagine it is a Friday night and tomorrow you are running onto the MCG to play the Grand Final.

That tomorrow is your big day. And how would you feel?

'He said, 'I would feel anxious.' Moshe asked, 'Yes, but what else? He replied he'd feel excited. Moshe explained this is the other part of it, that is what a lot of psychology does not do. It does not allow the person to look at the other side. It is anxiety, but on the other side of anxiety, the other side of the same coin, is also excitement.

'Jamie, if, as I think you still hope and I hope for you, that you get married one day…'

I laughed. 'Yes, Moshe you'll come to my Chuppah; I'll force you.'

Moshe asked, 'How will you feel the night before?'

'Terrified, I should imagine, and very excited, hopefully.'

'Then one day you will expect a child,' Moshe said.

'Oh, my word!' was my response.

'Will you be anxious?'

'Yes, very much.'

'Will you be excited?'

'Oy vey, I don't know.'

'I hope for your sake, and I would expect you would be. To miss out on anxiety,' he continued, 'is to miss out on life. It is part of being human. If you were satisfied that you were writing a book now, and it gets released, and tomorrow morning you expected Saturday's *Age* to have a review of your book, would you be anxious?'

'Moshe, can you imagine how much therapy I'd need!'

'That's good, it's wonderful,' he said. 'I'll have to live for many more years. What I am saying is this. Anxiety is human. The more things are important to us the more anxious we become. Anxiety is an aspect of caring, anxiety is an aspect of excitement. Anxiety is who you are, it is part of you and not to be anxious is not human.'

Anyone who knows me, knows that adult dating is something that gives me the most anxiety possible. I can't do it. I'm not interested. It's not for me. What am I supposed to say on a date? Why would I waste my time with a stranger? What if I see someone I know when I'm on a date? And so it goes on.

Funnily enough, while my mum always says that most of the things you worry about don't happen, one of the above did happen to me and it resulted in a very funny therapy session. For some reason, something that really worries me about being on a date is bumping into someone I know, and I have spent a lot of time thinking about how horrendous that would be for me. Especially if it was a family friend or adult, as opposed to one of my friends. Well, one day I was going on a second or third date with a very age-appropriate Jewish man from Melbourne who, on paper, ticked lots of boxes, and I was going crazy about it. He said he would pick me up and that we go to the beach for sunset, which I was very happy with. I assumed we would just go down to the beach near me, but he said his favourite place was further away, so off we went. I was happy about this. Thinking, perfect, even better to go further away with less chance of seeing someone I know. We arrived, got out of his car and walked down to the beach, where I noticed a group of about thirty adults and children. As we got closer, a man from the group shouted my nickname and thought I was hearing things.

When we got closer, more of them started shouting my name and saying hello and I realised it was my mum's husband's entire friendship group having dinner on the beach, at the same time I was there on an adult date! My worst nightmare came true. I did not know where to put myself, sort of said 'Hi' and ran away. I didn't introduce him and as we walked away, I couldn't help myself and said, 'Oh my word, this is so awkward! They are all going to know I'm on a date.' He let me know I could have said he was just a friend. Under any other circumstances I would have been really happy to see this group of family friends and probably would have joined them for a drink.

At our next session I told Moshe my worst nightmare came true. I was so traumatised. He didn't really get it. In essence, girls my age should want to date and be happy to be on a date, but to me it was overwhelming and scary. He explained to me that, back in the day when he was young, on a Saturday night if a young woman didn't have a date people felt sorry for her, whereas here I was sitting telling him how embarrassed I felt that people knew I was on a date. I still laugh about this story and Moshe's puzzled face. I also laugh about it with my family friends who know me well and know how friendly I usually would have been.

While I don't think I would be described as an anxious person, boys, men, dating, and relationships make me go crazy. But in one particular session, Moshe nudged and explored other areas in my life that have made me feel anxious.

*

Moshe Jamie, tell me about times when you have felt anxious in your life.

Jamie I'm not really the most anxious person, minus dating.

Moshe Yes, but you must have felt anxious before, tell me about it.

*

I couldn't really understand why he was so interested in knowing about other areas where I have felt anxious, because in my mind I was able to overcome them, but I told him I could think of two main areas. I didn't think it was necessary to spend time discussing them, but I went with it as Moshe seemed quite persistent.

The first, I explained was that I am anxious about going to the gym. In my mind I had made up stories: I'm not fit. I'm not Sporty Spice. Everyone else at the gym is better than me. I don't know what I'm doing. I'm bad at gym. Funnily enough, several of my very close friends are extremely fit, have six packs and exercise most days, and I have come to accept that is just not me. But I like the gym and exercising, especially yoga and weights, and I have consistently worked out for years.

*

Moshe So what did you do about going to the gym, how did you get over it?

Jamie I just went to gym. I went to the places with very fit people. I did the classes and asked for as much help as I could. I stopped caring about the other people there and just did my best.

Moshe Okay, and what is the other area you've faced anxiety about?

Jamie The working. My first year of work as a registered psychologist was equally anxiety-provoking and rewarding. I constantly felt inadequate, nervous, like I had absolutely no idea what I was doing and could not understand how my clients could possibly trust me to see them. I almost felt bad and that it wasn't fair to them. I would run into my psychology mentor's office asking questions basically before and after every client I saw. Not once did she make me feel like a burden or annoying. I planned and prepared as much as I could and, as with the gym, I just did my best.

*

Moshe made me feel so much better about this when he said, 'Well, Jamie, when you are treating children, diagnosing and completing such complex assessments, it is good that you are anxious and it is good that you ask for help because it is a serious matter, it shows that you are responsible.'

*

Moshe So would you say your anxiety made you work harder?

Jamie Yes, definitely, because I had to be more prepared to manage my own anxiety. I remember for that first year of work that I was so overwhelmed from my work week I spent several Saturday nights at home on my own, much to the dismay of my friends.

Moshe And what else has made you more at ease with the

anxiety of working?

Jamie I think time. I can't say to someone like you that I am an experienced psychologist, but I don't feel as fresh now as I did then. Most of the assessments I complete now I have more or less seen before, and not every session feels as new and scary as it did then. Also, I have slowly learnt to believe in myself more. I don't necessarily think I am a good psychologist, but I do everything I can to be the best and am trying every day to be more confident in myself and what I am doing.

*

At this point in the session, I was starting to feel kind of proud or happy about the way I had overcome these two significant obstacles in my life, but I still couldn't understand why I had to spend the hour telling Moshe about them. And then his simple yet incredible wisdom came out.

*

Moshe Well Jamie, it seems like you have done a very good job at overcoming these areas of anxiety in your life, and if you could do it with them then I believe you can do it with dating and relationships too.

*

Wow! I thought.

CHAPTER 4

From Small Talk to Medium Talk

My approach to writing this book has been somewhat similar to my approach to being in therapy. I went to the first session, spoke honestly and openly and acknowledged my difficulties, but much of the discussions for the first year or so were quite *surface* level. We discussed my family, my story and my work and life in general, and it took me a long time to trust enough to be able to change things from 'small talk to medium talk,' as Larry David (of *Curb Your Enthusiasm* fame) would say. As I have written this book, I have acknowledged my need for therapy, my need for help, my disappointments with life and anxieties with men and relationships as openly and honestly as I could, but I haven't elaborated or shared my full story.

Taking things to the next level is very confronting and difficult for everyone. I can't remember the context of the session, but I remember Moshe saying to me, after months of sessions, he noticed a difference in me and that I started talking much more openly.

Moshe had mentioned at the start of his talk to the school parents that he was a psychotherapist, and I never knew he was one or even what a psychotherapist opposed to a psychologist was. While one of my strengths as a psychologist would be my warm nature and personality, one of my weaknesses would be my knowledge of formal phrases, words and sometimes even the simplest of ideas – especially relating to myself.

I thought I had a lightbulb moment, early on in my therapy, saying, 'Oh, my goodness, Moshe, do you think I have issues with relationships and dating because of the difficulties I have faced in the relationship with my dad?' I was so excited I had pieced it together.

Moshe replied, 'Jamie, where did you train to be a psychologist? I am concerned about what you were taught, because that is one of the most basic ideas and theories in psychology. *Of course* it has.'

And we laughed.

As I wrote this book, I Googled the difference between counselling and psychotherapy and the answer I found: Counselling is a brief treatment that targets a specific symptom or situation, while psychotherapy is a longer-term treatment that attempts to gain more insight into someone's problems.

The latter is exactly what Moshe and I do and it is just so much fun. While many of the topics we discussed were serious and deeply difficult for me, Moshe has the best way of bringing humour into the space, whenever it is appropriate, which makes the process feel much less confronting and more manageable, even enjoyable.

While I believe my friends would describe me as a happy, bubbly person, I experience very strong emotions and feel things much more deeply than most people would realise. According to Moshe I am an 'extremely emotional person'. I think I have spent a lot of my life letting things bubble inside and not acknowledging my real feelings to myself, never mind to those around me.

In my training year as a psychologist, I learnt about communication training and how to teach it to children. We explain to them that there are those people who are like a jellyfish. They are passive and agreeable in order to avoid conflict, but often don't get what they want, feel resentful and can sometimes have outbursts and sting people. There are those who are like sharks, aggressive and bullying to others. Sharks often do get what they want, but they don't make meaningful connections because everyone just wants them to go away. And then there are those who are like dolphins, people who communicate assertively, which is the most empowering way of communicating, even if they don't get their desired outcome.

I FEEL...	Hurt and annoyed
WHEN...	You call me manipulative
BECAUSE...	I'm not trying to be manipulative
AND I'D LIKE...	You to try and hear what I am saying and please respect my needs

I teach and practise this assertive communication with children but communicating assertively has not been one of my own strengths. When reflecting, growing up I was very much like a jellyfish, not only in my communication with others but also in my communication with myself. I was happy-bubbly-Jamie who was doing well and fine and I never stopped to process what I had been through or how I was feeling about it. And as I am extremely emotional, the feelings were big.

That was probably my greatest gift from COVID and speaking to Moshe Lang. It has given me the power and the time to acknowledge my true feelings, insecurities, fears, anxieties, strengths and quirks, which for some silly reason caused me a lot of shame.

And so, the medium talk begins.

CHAPTER 5
Communication

Having written about different communication styles, honest communication is something I struggle with. I don't know how to say what I want to say. And when I do know what I want to say, I'm often not brave enough to say it. Communication is something that is important in all areas of life, and something that Moshe continually encourages me to do, openly and honestly, of course.

At one stage I had an annoying school-girl crush on a man who I would have described as a ladies' man. He was handsome, funny and kind – and a lot older than me. I had always felt a connection with him and noticed the way he looked at me, but in my mind, I thought there would be no way he would be into me, and he probably liked very skinny, fit, blonde girls. Well, I was wrong about that. Our interactions were fun, flirty, yet confusing for me. After a time, our night together finally came. Just the two of us and I was so excited. My friends had heard about this stupid crush for months, and they were excited for me too. I was going to have so much to tell them the next morning!

How wrong I was. I woke to lots of messages from my

friends, and eventually, after I left his place, had a video call with three of them. Of course, they wanted to know everything and all I had to tell them was that we had great cuddles. I was truly perplexed. I couldn't believe how close to and far away from what I wanted I had been, and neither could my girlfriends. Looking back now I can't believe I even spent time talking to Moshe about this man, but at the time I was so frazzled. We had such chemistry, but nothing happened.

Moshe casually and calmly suggested, I simply ask him his reasoning and why he didn't want to have sex with me. Again, simple, but it was so scary to me. It's now years later and we are still friends, and I still haven't been able to ask him that question. I also still really want to know the answer.

As a 29-year-old female, talking to your 83-year-old male psychologist about sex is slightly awkward, no matter what. I just don't see any situation where it wouldn't be a bit weird. But time and time again, Moshe tells me his job is to make me feel so comfortable that I can speak to him about anything and everything. He did his job so well, and while romance and intimacy comfortably and appropriately came up on occasion, the only thing I now try to keep on a small-talk level with Moshe and medium-talk level with my friends is sex.

Coming back to communication, there is one conversation I had with my dad that I slightly cringe about.

*

Jamie   Dad, I've started seeing a psychologist.

Dad   Oh Jamie, that's nice. Why?

Jamie   Because I have so many problems.

Dad   Do you really, doll? What are all of your problems about?

Jamie   You!

*

Looking back at this conversation I see how young and immature I was. I think this was one of the things you're supposed to think and not say, but I said it. And now, after a lot of self-growth and exploration, journal-writing, tears and laughs – I understand that all of these *problems* have actually been my greatest *lessons* and will continue to be for the rest of my life. Also, I have come to realise the problems aren't about my dad, they are my own problems that I need to figure out and make peace with on my own. I have the choice to lead a life the way I want to live, something which my very special naturopath told me quite strongly one day.

Both of my parents have told me that one day you have to get over your parents and one day you have to get over your children. And that is something I have worked on the most with Moshe. He guided me in letting go of who I thought my father should be and how I think he should act and accept him for who he is – one of my favourite people in the whole world, with qualities that I admire greatly, who also drives me the most insane.

*

Moshe   It is part of the process of growing up. You separate from your parents. And Jamie, very few parents are perfect. They all have shortcomings. When I say shortcomings, they may be shortcomings in your mind, not in other people's minds, but in that sense, you are the important one. Your parents have shortcomings, and you learn to accept it, one way or another.

Jamie   They are what they are.

Moshe   They are what they are, and it is what you have.

*

"You have to try to be happy with what you've got. Life is wonderful if you're happy. Don't look on the other side of the fence. You will never be happy if you look at your neighbour and make yourself sick with jealousy."
—Eddie Jaku, *The Happiest Man on Earth*

Moshe said that this was a process that happens to all children at one stage, and it can be very difficult. I certainly found it difficult. I had so many sessions in which I would walk into Moshe's office feeling like I was about to cry and trying to hold it back.

*

Moshe   How are you today, Jamie?

Jamie   Fine, thanks.

Moshe   Your face tells me something different.

*

Sessions like these mainly occurred in our second year of therapy. I had the worst fight with my dad I had ever had and this triggered a downward spiral in which I felt lonely, sad and hurt. I think at that time I was just floating through each day feeling a bit lost, and I wasn't myself. I didn't like my life – I thought it was boring, and that the only thing I had going on was my work. The only person who knew the real extent of the pain I was feeling was Moshe, and he supported me so safely during that time. I trusted him and honestly communicated how I was feeling and what was going on for me. It wasn't rainbows and butterflies and fairies, and Moshe didn't try to 'fix' me, change me or change the situation, he just sat in it with me. More *growing pains*.

Another form of communication Moshe has encouraged me to do when I am feeling anxious is to express it, as a way of releasing some of the anxiety.

*

Jamie Moshe, I might be going on a date tonight. I'm freaking out.

Moshe Why don't you tell the man you are so anxious about dating and just be honest. He will know you are anxious by your behaviour, and once you say it you might feel much less anxious.

Jamie No way.

*

I did finally take this advice though; it was at a time when I gave a presentation on Autism Spectrum Disorder for a school staff. On the one hand I couldn't understand why they would want a presentation from me and not someone more experienced, and on the other hand it was an honour to be asked to do it. Every part of me wanted to say no, because it felt so terrifying and out of my comfort zone, but I knew deep inside me I had to do it. And I did.

I started like this:

'Hello – thanks so much for having me here today. Over the years I have had the chance to work with many of you, but for anyone that doesn't know me, my name is Jamie Maserow. It is a privilege to be standing here today to talk for the next hour about Autism Spectrum Disorder. When I was asked to give this presentation, my first thought was no, I definitely don't know enough about Autism Spectrum Disorder to be able to complete a presentation on it, and my second thought was that there is absolutely no way I can public speak in front of an audience for an hour. But if I spend my days trying to promote a growth mindset in children, whereby I teach them that hard things grow our brain, challenges make us stronger and it doesn't matter if we make a mistake, then I had to practice what I preach and say yes. I am most definitely not an expert on Autism Spectrum Disorder, but I am going to do my best to teach you the most I can in the next hour...'

Honest and straightforward communication.
Thanks, Moshe, it made the presentation slightly easier.

CHAPTER 6

Bringing a Family Member to Therapy

'Jamie, it's not normal how much you talk about your psychologist, Moshe Lang. You never stop talking about him. What's wrong with you?' This wasn't the first time someone asked me about Moshe Lang.

*

Jamie   You don't understand how clever he is and how good it is talking about my problems with him. It's so much fun.

Mum   Jamie, I want to come and meet him. I need to meet this man.

Jamie   Why do you need to meet my psychologist? That's not normal and it's not like we have any particular problems that we need him to help us with together.

Mum   Because your face lights up every time you speak about him, and he is just someone I want to meet.

Jamie   Okay, I'll talk to him about it, but it's so weird, Mum.

*

Several weeks after this conversation I received another phone call from someone who has been part of my life since

I was around nine years old. One of my favourite people in the world. We couldn't be more different, but we have always had a special bond.

'Jamie, I need to tell you something. I have been researching Moshe Lang all night and I just need to see him. I don't need a psychologist, like I don't think I need therapy and don't know what I would talk to him about, but I think he is the only psychologist in the world I could speak to, and I want to speak to him.'

I was so excited and knew the two of them would get on so well, and after his first session he told me, 'We spent the entire session sharing and finishing each other's jokes — it was so much fun, but Moshe said I really need to find some reasons to see him besides the Yiddish jokes.'

In most of Moshe's sessions at the start he would often tell me jokes. And while I love a laugh, I just don't understand jokes and never find them funny. I tried to be polite at the start and would fake giggle, but I guess my face showed Moshe otherwise. Without me needing to tell him, he stopped telling me these jokes because I never laughed when I am supposed to and often do when I am not supposed to.

Moshe once mentioned to me that he often sees the parents of people my age for therapy to discuss how they wish their child would be partnered with someone Jewish. However, by the time the children are in their mid to late thirties, their parents don't care anymore and just want them to be married and not single. When he told me this, I found it very funny, and still do, and Moshe looked at me and said, 'Jamie, it's not funny at all. It's very hard for the parents. It is a serious problem.'

A few months later I asked how he was going with Moshe, and he said it was great but he didn't really need it anymore and Moshe agreed, so they had decided to stop his sessions. As he told me this, I had a strong feeling inside me, but I can't describe what it was – if I had to choose a word, I would call it envy. At that time I thought I was doing so well that I was about to suggest to Moshe that we should change to monthly rather than fortnightly sessions, but before I suggested it, he looked at me and said, 'Jamie, if time wasn't a factor for me and money wasn't a factor for you, ideally I would like to see you every week, but we will make do with every fortnight.' Oy vey, things were worse than I thought – I still laugh about this every time I think of it.

Since then, I found something very validating, describing the difference between envy and jealousy, in Brené Brown's *Atlas of the Heart*. This wonderful book describes in depth the eighty-seven emotions and experiences that humans face. Brené writes that she wants the book, 'to be an atlas for all of us because… with an adventurous heart and the right maps, we can travel anywhere and never fear losing ourselves.' Brené explains how important language is in helping us to make meaning of events in our lives, to connect, heal, learn and become self-aware. Understanding the correct language to use gives us more power. Two examples that particularly stood out to me were: Envy occurs when we want something that another person has and jealousy is when we fear losing a relationship or a valued part of a relationship that we already have.

When I heard he didn't need therapy anymore, I was thrilled for him, but I wanted to be in a place when I didn't have *problems,* and I didn't need therapy anymore. But I knew I still needed it, and so I felt envious.

My family is very traditional, and Friday night is the time we come together over dinner and talk. Often something will come up and he'll look at me with his beaming eyes and ask, 'What would Moshe say?' When I told him about the idea of the book, he described Moshe well and said, 'You know, Jamie, he is just one of those people with a great spirit – he just has a great spirit.'

And my mum is still dying to meet him. If she comes to a session with me before I finish this book, I will write about it, otherwise maybe she can meet him at the book launch.

CHAPTER 7

Thick Skin

I will never forget the session with Moshe when I told him I had a new romantic interest who was considerably younger than me. I really liked him, but deep down I knew that it wasn't going to go anywhere.

*

Jamie   Moshe, it's amazing and fun and I feel so happy, but I could never expect him to settle down. It's not fair – I remember what I was doing when I was his age.

Moshe   Yes, I understand, but another way to see it is how lucky he would be to shape his young adulthood with someone like you by his side.

*

Moshe has said several kind things to me over the years but for some reason this one really stood out. Another session I remember very clearly was during lockdown, when I was sitting in my car, at the beach, talking to Moshe on the phone. I don't know how it came up, but basically, I told him that a few times a week I get kind compliments, but I sort of brushed them off and didn't really believe them. Moshe questioned me a lot about this and made me tell him the types of compliments I'd received. I actually had to say the words out loud to him. It was a nightmare. I remember my face being bright red throughout the conversation. I was sweating so much that I had to have the air conditioner on full blast. This is one session I was so happy to be having via telehealth – I don't think I could have had it face-to-face. Moshe explained there is a clear difference between being humble and not arrogant, and not seeing the positive qualities in yourself that other people do.

It has taken me so much time, but I now feel more confident in myself and less insecure. It is a very nice feeling. *Maybe even some of those compliments are true!*

Moshe has also made me feel better about some things I have thought about my family, and some things I have said out loud to them. In one session I told him an outrageous comment I had said a year or two earlier. It was about a completely made-up scenario in my mind that would have a one-in-a-million chance of occurring.

*

Moshe The way I understand it, a common thing that any child asks themselves is, do you love me, don't you love me, or do you love me more than you love someone else? Whether they say it or not, it is a question people ask themselves all the time.

Jamie Moshe, my brother looked at me as if I was quite insane.

Moshe Well I don't think so. It is the other way around. You suffer from excessive normalcy. Put it in your book as my diagnosis, Jamie. It's a great diagnosis!

*

Another session, however, was very frustrating. I really didn't want to go to – not because of what I had to discuss, but rather because I was mentally and physically exhausted. I was burnt out for the first time in my psychology career and had no space for my clients and no space for myself. My cup was either empty or overflowing, I'm not sure which. I wasn't sad, I just felt 'done' and concerned about how I would get through the next fortnight of work and life before my summer holidays began. I didn't cancel the session because I never do, and I remember it being very annoying. Moshe questioned and probed me about a touchy subject and was probably disappointed in my lack of communication about it. He was probably also shocked, because in some ways my communication had been improving, but in this instance it hadn't at all. I ended the session feeling a bit rattled, but I had already been rattled from the start, so the session had just added to it.

I told Moshe I had no space for therapy and didn't want to come to my next fortnightly session.

'Don't cancel your next session, because it is one of the ways you take care of yourself. Don't neglect yourself right now when you need it the most. I think it is very important you make time for it.'

I agreed, even though I wasn't happy about it, but I had no space or energy to argue with him. I ended up getting COVID a few days later, so I didn't have to worry about the next fortnight of a full calendar, and in the ten days of isolation I managed to clear my mind and process that session.

*

Jamie Moshe, I couldn't even listen or take in what you were saying to me last time because my mind was so full, but now I understand it more because I have had the space and time to be able to process it.

Moshe I thought about it after you walked out of the room and wondered if I had been too harsh on you.

Jamie Look, Moshe, I think you were too harsh for my frame of mind that week. I just needed a soft, kind session, and it was too much for me to hear at the time because I was just so full and overwhelmed, but now I can really appreciate and understand what you were trying to explore with me.

Moshe Yes, Jamie, that's what I meant. Part of being a good psychologist is reflecting on your work and realising when you make mistakes or can do things better, and admitting it.

Jamie Don't worry, I have thick skin. It will take a lot more than you telling me the truth and being blunt for me to leave and not want to come back, and now I can see exactly what you were trying to say!

*

I went on to tell him my COVID story. Moshe and I had a very deep conversation and when I checked it with him for this book, I thought he would remember it word for word.

*

Moshe Jamie you are giving me credit that I do not deserve.

If you think I remember everything I say, you are silly.

*

We both laughed loudly and continued arguing about me thinking he would remember and him telling me clearly that he didn't.

*

Moshe In any human relationship you can be overly kind, and just bullshit and disrespect the person that way. Or you can be too harsh, or you can be just right. How do you bloody know? You do your best and it is partially modest, you could call it modest or realistic. You do your best and you may have misjudged. You may have misjudged because you are hungry or tired or whatever. Sometimes the harshness in retrospect could be a very good thing for you and me. I have experienced moments in my life that were tough. I was in the army in Israel where there was a Hebrew word, a euphemism for the fact that they were really torturing us. Some people with me… I remember one who committed suicide… he couldn't take it. And others who survived it and as a result are bigger and better. Just to be clear, it may be that I was insensitive, or not sufficiently sensitive, or too harsh, but it's not the end of the world if I was. When you work well with people you sometimes overshoot the mark or undershoot the mark. I'll give you the yoga metaphor. When you stretch in yoga, you know that it is very difficult to make the judgement of how far you will stretch before you tear a muscle or strain too much. You can overdo it, and you can underdo it and you can just get it right. But how do you know what's right? It is a feeling. The best part you see is that months later we are still talking, and we can laugh and argue and smile together about it.

CHAPTER 8

My Covid Story

I have been told many times that my life is like a movie or that I need my own reality TV show, but I think this next story is one of my best. And while there are some very sad and scary parts to it, I am so grateful for the way things turned out because I spent the first three days of isolation in my bed crying with laughter as opposed to crying with anxiety about the fact that not only had I contracted, but passed on the dreaded virus, at a time when every single case was reported on the news in Melbourne.

One Friday afternoon, I went to meet a close friend whose partner was in hospital. We had a very quick coffee, and he asked what I was doing the following night, a Saturday night. I said nothing and suggested he came over so that he wasn't alone. He was happy and said OK, and that he'd tell our other friends to come too. I, for some reason, decided I would cook dinner because I hadn't ever had them over for dinner. I then went to a Friday night family dinner with my extended family, where I shared dessert with my Bobba and sat opposite a couple who are both Holocaust survivors.

I love entertaining and friends being at my house,

but cooking is not one of my fortes. Usually it is gins, cheeseboards, corn chips and dips. The following day came, and I remember feeling exhausted, but I thought it was due to a busy week and went about preparing for the dinner. My friend called me again and had invited two more of our friends, so there would be six of us in total.

I remember this friend once telling me he would be very scared staying at his home on his own, so I suggested he sleep over in my spare room so that he didn't have to go home alone while his partner was in hospital. He appreciated the offer and said he would stay after dinner. I was excited we were all going to have a very fun night. I wanted to make everything nice. I set the table and tried to make it look as pretty as I could with candles, flowers and a black tablecloth. I decided I wouldn't drink that night because I was feeling so exhausted and imagined it being a very chilled night. I made fish tacos with great fish from the frozen section in Coles that you put in the oven. This friend still teases me that the dinner didn't count as cooking because I didn't make the fish myself, but that is way too much cooking for me.

About half an hour after everyone arrived, I received a text message saying, 'Hey,' from the housemate of two of our friends who were at my dinner. I had met him a couple of times before and he had given me his cute jumper with daisies on it after I told him I liked it. I wasn't sure if this was flirting or not but when I messaged him to say thank you, he said it was a pleasure and asked if I had received any compliments on the jumper and following this, we hadn't had any further communication. Actually, I sent him a selfie in his jumper which he didn't respond to, but for some weird reason, the second I got his 'Hey' message I knew something was going to happen. I invited him to come over, and about twenty minutes later he arrived. The night ended up being fun and I had quite a few gins. I had no appetite (now I understand why – thanks, COVID) and got quite tipsy. Everyone was getting on well, conversation was flowing, and my friends seemed to be enjoying the night, even if the fish came from the frozen section in Coles.

Daisy boy and I had great banter and conversations throughout the night and before I knew it was close to midnight. All of a sudden, my friend who was supposed to sleep over stood up and said he was leaving with another friend. I remember standing at my front door arguing with him, saying, 'Oh my goodness, I was so excited for you to sleep over I even cleaned the spare room, please just stay – come on!' His answer was, 'Jimmy, I'm really tired and I just feel like going home.' I was kind of disappointed, but he seemed keen to go home so there was nothing I could do about it. Shortly after, another couple went home and after I had let them out, the other two housemates said they were leaving too. So, it was just Daisy boy and me. We continued to drink and shared a fun and unexpected night.

The following morning, I had a very big hangover and a very big day ahead, especially for a Sunday. It started with a stroll down the street and coffee with one of my friends from the dinner who had come back to pick up his car.

'What happened with you and Daisy boy?' he asked.

'Why do you ask?'

'You guys had such chemistry the entire night it was so obvious to all of us. He didn't talk to anyone except you the whole night.'

I found out that everyone had purposefully left in stages so that he would be left with me, and there wouldn't be an awkward moment where everyone was leaving, and he had to either stay or leave. What thoughtful friends! The second my friend said there was obvious chemistry between us I immediately felt embarrassed. *Oh no! Did I seem to like him too much? Did I spend too much time with him at the dinner? Did I seem too keen?* but all I responded to my friend was, 'What do you mean, could you really tell?'

I spoke to the friend who was supposed to sleep over on the phone. I told him how disappointed I was that he didn't.

'Jamie, I was actually being a good friend. I didn't want to be a cock block and purposefully left, so you should thank me.'

I truly couldn't believe it.

Following the coffee, I proceeded to attend a first birthday party, a Christmas party at a busy bar, my friend's pool for an hour, and then home for a power nap and off to a delicious Japanese restaurant for dinner with another friend. Funnily enough I went back to the restaurant with the same friend and came home to write this story. For me, or anyone, it was a very busy and social day. At dinner I laughed with my friend about how busy my Sunday was. He knows me well and that it is rare for me to be so social. The entire day I wasn't feeling great, but it made sense as I'd had a very late night, and I definitely did not feel sick.

The following morning, I walked down to the beach for two hours on my own to process my big weekend. I was coughing a little bit and didn't feel great, but again I wasn't surprised after the weekend I'd had. As I was getting ready for work, I saw a rapid antigen test kit sitting on the table and for some reason, I thought I should do the test to be sure I was clear before going to the office at 12 pm. One of my greatest anxieties has been to be the one that brought COVID to the office. I knew no one would judge or blame me, but I really was quite paranoid about it. I did the test and thought it was okay, then as I was leaving looked again, and it had changed (it had been more than thirty minutes). I felt confused and decided to stop at the pharmacy on the way to my office and do another one to be safe.

I made it to the pharmacy by 11.45 am, bought two rapid tests and sat in my car outside the office as I waited for the fifteen minutes. I saw my 12 pm client walk into the building. I called reception and said I should be up in fifteen minutes at 12.00, unless I tested positive, but I really didn't think I would be. The fifteen minutes passed and both rapid tests clearly had two strong red lines. I called reception to tell her the outcome and I felt so bad about the timing and having to cancel my client's appointment, but they were very understanding of the situation.

I remember calling my mum straight away to tell her, still not believing I had COVID, and she said, 'Yes, you probably do.'

*

Jamie Mum, should I tell my friends or wait for the proper test – I don't want to freak anyone out unnecessarily, but one has been going into the hospital every day and I just don't know what to do!

Mum I just don't know – you should tell him, maybe just tell your friends to take a rapid and be mindful this week.

Jamie I had the busiest weekend of my life, and there are so many people I need to tell – you don't even understand.

Mum Jamie, you age me!

*

While my greatest fear was bringing COVID to the office, I am so grateful that never happened, but my very social weekend had significant ramifications for several people. This part is not a blessing of the pandemic. I believe one at the hospital went into a lockdown until my friend who had visited the hospital the following day tested negative. I then had to call Daisy boy and tell him I probably had COVID. How do things like this even happen to me? He had gone away with his family, and I believe they ended up having to isolate for a week too because he had spent a significant amount of time with them. He ended up testing positive.

'Was it worth it?' I asked him.

'Absolutely not,' he said, and we both laughed over the phone. I then told him how everyone had set it up and that they planned to leave in stages so things wouldn't be awkward between the two of us.

'I know, I asked them to, I was in on it.'

I couldn't believe it. Sometimes I am so naïve!

His housemate also tested positive, and so did my friend whose pool I'd visited on the Sunday afternoon. From my experience, making people sick is one of the worst feelings possible. It is different to intentionally doing wrong by someone, and while I still find this story funny, my heart was in pain knowing that these people were sick and isolating for ten days because of me. It was a physical feeling inside my body.

Throughout the time I felt an immense amount of love and support from everyone around me. Not one person made me feel slightly bad, and everyone tried to make me feel better about the situation.

'Jamie, it's not your fault.'

'It's a bad situation but no one's fault.'

'It's not like you knew you had it and still had us over.'

'JAMIE, STOP SAYING SORRY!!!'

Even when I told them all I had tested positive and they were in a scary position themselves, wondering if they would test positive or not, every friend asked if I was okay or needed anything. Later that afternoon on the day I tested positive I received the most beautiful hamper from the ladies at the office.

An interesting part of this is how much I enjoyed the mandated ten days of isolation. It was a blessing in disguise. I stayed in my dressing gown the entire time, slept when I wanted to, did a couple of important zoom appointments, took supplements and herbs every two hours and rested from a very busy year. When I had the energy, I spent hours on the phone to friends telling them the funny story. My mum was an angel and bought me everything I asked for so kindly. And my requests aren't simple, I like specific things from specific places and not once was it too much trouble for her. I also spent hours on Facetime with my good friends from the dinner party, who spent several anxious days when two of the others tested positive – they were all waiting for their turn.

We also had a Facetime video call on the Friday night as everyone was banished from their family dinners in case they had the virus, and I realised this was the first Friday night in my entire life I had ever spent alone. While many more people in Melbourne had COVID by then, at the time not many people did, and I remember my brother checking in with me on the phone saying, 'Jamie, it's actually so scary my sister has COVID, I can't believe it.'

Healthwise, I was sick and quite knocked out, but I have been sicker before in my life. My sleeping patterns were strange, and I had a temperature for about the first three days. At the start I kept thinking, *If I stay like this, I will be fine.* I guess the scary thing about COVID was that it could get much worse and you didn't know how it was going to hit you.

When I told Moshe this story from isolation, he said he enjoyed how much joy I got from the story and suggested I write it down. He could hear it in my voice over the phone. I wrote it in the yellow journal beside my bed. I wrote about how all my friends said if Daisy boy and I got married, it would make for the best wedding speech and love story ever. And when I told Moshe about Daisy boy and how that had played out, he said, 'Jamie, can't you see what went on here? All your friends noticed the connection between the two of you, but you could not admit to yourself that you were interested in him.'

CHAPTER 9
The L Word

The most beautiful and long-lasting love story I have ever witnessed in my life is that of my grandparents, Fran and Dennis. It is like a movie, a fairy-tale love story that has lasted for sixty-one years. It gives me the most joy when I visit them unexpectedly and walk up their driveway to hear them sitting on the couch laughing together or see them playing Scrabble or eating together. My Zaida still stands at the door to let my Bobba in before him, and my Bobba still comes home every day to make Zaida a sandwich for lunch and sets his clothes out on their bed for the day. It is real, it is pure, and it is wonderful. And it is an example of love that Moshe continually encourages me to look up to.

*

Jamie   Moshe, I don't even understand why I have such relationship problems and why I take rejection so badly. I have had only one proper boyfriend, but several flings, and while I have been very disappointed in how some have turned out, I don't think I could say I have had my heart truly broken.

Moshe   I understand, but you've had your heart broken by the most important man in your life.

Jamie My dad. (I remember getting a lump in my throat then, but I don't think I properly cried.)

*

It is very interesting that our brains are wired to think negatively. It stems from caveman days when life was dangerous, and cavemen were often in fight or flight mode because of real danger, and not because of their thoughts. If they went into a cave and saw a lion, they would get eaten and die, so they had to make sure not go into the cave again to stay alive. Often, they would replay such an event over and over in their minds. This thinking pattern has been passed on through generations, and is our brain's way of protecting us, of trying to keep us safe, although it causes us significant suffering when we are not often in physical danger. I learnt this idea from Russ Harris, a life coach, medical practitioner and psychotherapist who has written several books and created courses for psychologists to learn Acceptance and Commitment Therapy. If you are interested in learning more about it, I recommend watching his *Caveman Mind* YouTube video. It goes for three minutes and explains this idea better than I have in this paragraph. It is brilliant!

The reason I am sharing it is because although I have so many beautiful examples of love stories around me, I have become scared of romantic love because I focus on what happened to my parents.

*

Jamie They were a dream couple and look how that ended.
Moshe Yes, I understand, but look at your grandparents.

*

In my conversations with Moshe, we say, 'the L word' instead of 'love'.

*

Moshe Jamie, might I, G-d forbid, suggest you love him?

*

This same boy Moshe was referring to went away for some time, and I replayed some of a phone conversation we'd had to Moshe.

*

Jamie Moshe, he said he misses me. Can you believe it?

Moshe And what did you say?

Jamie I said I miss him too, even though I hate to admit it.

Moshe Of course you miss him, it is so normal for you to miss him. It is someone you have spent a lot of time with over the last few months, and now he is away. There's nothing wrong with missing him.

Jamie Oh my goodness, Moshe, do you think he knows I like him?

Moshe Jamie, for such an intelligent young woman you baffle me sometimes!

*

One thing I have realised in reflecting on my therapy is how Moshe has tried to help me understand the way my behaviour may come across to the men I interact with. I am most often so anxious about it that my behaviour is much more guarded and closed off than I intend it to be, and sometimes Moshe tries to highlight this to me. I think this is helpful, because I tend to focus on how they come across to me, rather than the other way around.

A funny example of this was when I was discussing with Moshe an upcoming wedding which I wasn't thrilled about attending. In my mind I had built it up to be a very big deal, felt intimidated by the thought of the crowd and insecure about going on my own when most people my age would be in couples, if not already married. But I told Moshe proudly, 'I have given strict instructions to my family that they are not allowed to leave my side, so I will actually be fine.'

*

Moshe And Jamie, what if there is a nice, eligible single man for you to meet there?

Jamie Moshe, there won't be – trust me. (I scrunched my face up as I said this.)

Moshe And if there is, he will look over at you, and might think what an attractive young lady, but why has she been sitting with her mother the entire night, and he probably won't speak to you.

*

At the end of that session Moshe looked at me and said something along the lines of, 'It is actually unfair that I get paid to hear such stories, Jamie. Sometimes I think I shouldn't be getting paid for this.' And again he shook his head.

That night I picked up his book *Resilience* to review for my writing, and read the following words from Moshe on the back cover:

> People entrust me with their stories. I witness their courage and loyalty as well as their pain and distress. I am paid to take

part in and observe rich and complex human dramas as they unfold. Sometimes I think it is I who should pay.

CHAPTER 10

Becoming a Psychologist

I never wanted to be a psychologist. Growing up, I wanted to be a teacher. A primary-school classroom teacher, the one that everyone loves and remembers. And then by the time I finished VCE I wanted to be a fashion designer. I wanted to go to fashion school at RMIT University and I applied for that. Sometimes I still want that when I go shopping and can't find exactly what I want. But I didn't get in and for some reason started an Arts degree at Monash University where I did some psychology subjects and some criminology subjects, with the potential of moving into a law degree if my marks were high enough. As my first semester of university began, I immediately loved my psychology subjects and really did not enjoy the criminology subjects. It was then that I decided I wanted to be a psychologist.

The route to becoming a psychologist is not easy. After you finish your undergraduate degree, you need to get into honours. I took a year off after finishing my undergraduate degree and spent the first half of the year working and saving and the second half travelling. I went with my best friend from school to all the places that were on our bucket list, and it was the most incredible seven-month trip. We saw the ancient baths in Pamukkale, Turkey, went to Ultra festival in Croatia, Boom festival in Portugal, ate at the Hotel de Paris in Monte Carlo, pretended we were stewardesses at the Monaco yacht show, shopped in Milan and spent some months with our boyfriends living and working at a bar in London. I found this entry I wrote in my travel journal during the trip that describes the essence of what I was experiencing, highlighting how I have always enjoyed writing without knowing it.

> Journal Entry: How I feel right now – so so lucky. The past 11 weeks have been everything I have dreamed of and more. I often have to pinch myself to believe it's real and I am actually in and seeing all of the different places I have dreamed of going to. We have seen so much beauty and nature and I have loved every second of it. From the Dead Sea to Palmukkale, Santorini and Oia sunset, Florence River overlooking the whole town at night, Tuscan Vineyards, Cinque Terre hike through the mountains and finally to Boom, a magical, fairy, made-up land. It's crazy that I have almost been away for the same time I was working full time for. Time is going so quickly, but every day we do what we want, and it is just perfect. We laugh so much and have met such funny and fun and weird people, and it has just been such an experience. Everything is too good, and I am happy, lucky and grateful to be doing what I am.

As the trip came to an end, I wanted so badly to get into honours and was nervous about my marks. I remember finding out that I had been accepted into the graduate diploma and on the first day of this course the lecturers explained to us that basically none of us would get into the masters course to become registered psychologists. I couldn't believe it because at the time I thought the biggest hurdle was getting into honours. Why would they shut us down on our first day like this? Why did they not have faith in us?

Honours year was to me the most difficult in the psychology course and halfway through I got glandular fever and then chronic fatigue. My skin was a yellowish-grey, and each morning I felt as if I had been hit by a bus. Both Mum and Dad separately suggested that I defer the course that year to recover and complete the course the following year. They are not normally those kinds of parents, and they have bought us up to be resilient and encouraged us to work hard, and that sometimes it is OK for life to be hard. But in this case, I was very sick.

To me, however, that wasn't an option – it was such an annoying, competitive year I just needed to get it done and not have it weighing on my shoulders the following year. So, I wrote my thesis from my bed. When I did go into university, I was weak and timid. My Uni friends took great care of me. They would often send me home to rest. It was a very difficult three months.

I went to see a healer as I wasn't getting any better. On top of being unwell, being twenty-three and stuck at home every Saturday night for three months was very frustrating. I wanted to be out with my friends having fun, but I was stuck in my bed, unable even to go out for a casual dinner.

My healer told me very important words that have stuck with me to this day.

'Jamie, don't fight it. This is where you are meant to be right now. Just enjoy being in your bed on a Saturday night and make the most of it, listen to music or read a book – it won't last forever.'

I used these words a lot in the lockdowns when we were stuck at home. I would tell myself; this is where I am meant to be right now. Just make the most of it and enjoy it, don't fight it.

Every Saturday night in that three-month period when I was unwell, Mum and her husband invited their friends over to our house for takeaways. They would always get me food, too, and I would come downstairs for a short while and chat to whoever was there and eat dinner with them. It was nice at the time. But as I got better, I remember thinking to myself how strange it was that they didn't go out on Saturday nights anymore.

'Gees, Mum, you're really old now. You guys don't even go out on Saturday nights anymore. What's happened to you?'

She gave me a look and then it all came to me. She and her husband knew I would be home and unable to go out, so they had changed their arrangements on all those Saturday nights so that I wasn't alone.

'Yes Jamie, did you think I would actually go out and leave you in that state? By the way, you are so rude for saying we've become old for not going out anymore!'

And we cried with laughter. How loved and cared for I am, I thought after this conversation.

I remember going out with my friends after we had handed in our theses. I was feeling better, and we got quite drunk.

They were shocked at how much I enjoyed going out as they had only ever seen me weak, unwell and quiet.

To get into masters you need a high distinction and a score above 80, as well as considerable experience in psychology-related activities or work experience, an interview and generally to be older – they don't really like taking young students. Well, for my thesis I got 79. So typically me! And, looking back, I didn't get one high distinction in my entire degree, but consistently scored in the 70s. I was, however, determined to get straight into masters, as I had taken the previous year to travel and didn't want another year off. When there are 700 applications for twenty spots in masters, it is basically impossible, especially at the age of twenty-three. For some reason, I got two interviews and when I got accepted into a course, I asked the co-ordinator if there weren't many applications that year.

She looked at me, puzzled, and said, 'No, Jamie, there were hundreds. Why do you ask?'

'Because I got in, I just thought maybe this year there weren't as many applications as usual.'

She shook her head in an annoyed way when I made this comment – another example of how I have not been able to see the qualities in myself that others do.

I remember one class in masters when we were talking about birth order in a family and how that may affect one's development and personality. A few minutes into it, the entire class looked at me and said, 'You're definitely the baby, Jamie.' I laughed and replied that it may seem like that but actually I was the eldest, and my brother was five years younger than me, even though he was more like the older sibling. They couldn't believe it! My baby brother is someone I am so incredibly grateful to. Throughout all the hard times, the one thing I had that remained constant, no matter where we were, was him. When we first had to get used to living between our parent's homes, we were always together. I don't think I could have managed without him. I felt safe having him with me, and still do.

Even though we are very different in so many ways, the main things that bond us together are our core values. We both believe in Judaism, in family, in helping others and in achieving well in life. When we moved from New Zealand, he looked after us like a champion. Maybe that is why he has always seemed so grown up. He pushes me to be my best. I remember one night we were all in the kitchen late on a Saturday and he was quite drunk (which was a nice change, as usually it's me).

'Jamie, you are twenty-three now, you need to get your life together.'

'What do you mean, my life is together. I've just been accepted into masters, what else do you want from me?'

I still laugh about this. I think to him my life will only be together when I am married – well, he'll just have to keep waiting!

The process to become a registered psychologist is difficult and I don't like speaking about it with students who are in the process of doing honours/masters. I remember the stress, the pressure, how competitive it feels (I am not a competitive person at all). But when they ask me, I put a smile on my face and tell them it is hard, but it is so worth it in the end if you are passionate about it. You can't do it unless you are passionate, I don't think it would be possible.

When I was first registered as a twenty-five-year-old psychologist, I felt embarrassed to tell people what I did. Now I am proud of it. Being a psychologist is my calling, and something I am honoured to be. Sometimes it is easier to tell people I am a fashion designer. That is my go-to, because when I tell people I'm a psychologist their response is always 'Oh my goodness, are you analysing me right now?' or 'What am I thinking?' The truth is, I am a person too, and when I am not working, I am Jamie having fun.

Earlier on, when I was in a supervision session, I was introduced to Acceptance and Commitment Therapy and given Russ Harris' book, *The Happiness Trap*. I remember thinking to myself, Oh gosh, this is probably just another silly self-help book. I was wrong. I read the book by the time of our next supervision and besides it teaching me about how to help clients, I found it really helpful in learning about myself and my own life. I remember answering some questions in the book which allow you to figure out how you want to lead your life, what your work, health, personal and physical values are and then how to live by them. It was so helpful to me, and I think it changed my life a little bit.

Being a psychologist is something that is not easy, but I guess that in most things in life, to do well you have to work hard. While my friends love to tease me that 'I'm never at work' and 'I don't really work' because I am not in a 9-5 office and have one morning off. I feel like I have worked extremely hard and want to be the best psychologist I can be, and that is something I get from both of my parents – a strong work ethic.

My dad is one of the best examples I know of someone who didn't finish high school or university and has made a huge success of his career. When I asked him if he got expelled from school, he clarified with me that he got expelled three times. When he told me this I giggled and thought that if it was in today's world his parents would frantically be trying to get an appointment with someone like me. He, however, with the help of my mum, found his passion at nineteen years old and became an expert in his field. He is well known and well liked, and I hope one day to be half as good a psychologist as he is in his field. I truly admire his success and his brilliant work ethic.

My mum, too, is an independent woman who has provided beautifully for her children. She has a strong work ethic, an outstanding reputation in what she does and, like Dad, is well known and well liked. Most of the time when I bump into either my mother's employees or people she has worked with I always hear that she is just the best person and I'm so lucky to have her as my mum, and that they wished she was their mum. It makes me smile.

CHAPTER 11

Welcome to the Jungle

Growing up, I was never a girl who dreamed of getting married and having children. At one point – I am assuming it was after my parents split up – I said I didn't ever want to get married and have children. I couldn't understand why people would do it. My mum also told me that as a young girl I never played with dolls or dressed up as a bride and preferred arts and crafts.

I never particularly loved children either. When I was a teenage girl I did some babysitting occasionally, but it wasn't my favourite thing to do. I found children quite annoying, to be honest. There was one family whose youngest son didn't manage well with babysitters. For some reason, he managed well with me, and his parents were only comfortable leaving him with me. They were a very caring, loving family, and every few Saturday nights I would babysit for them. Once I received a call from the mother asking me to babysit at 9 am on a Sunday morning. Absolutely not I told her. I couldn't think of a worse way to spend my Sunday morning. She begged me, and basically told me I had to, and that no wasn't an option. The day came, I reluctantly arrived and put the Wiggles on for the youngest boy, and I think we both slept for a few hours that morning while the TV was on, his parents were out, and I was getting paid well. On reflection, although I sometimes found children annoying, maybe I was always able to interact well with them, even if I didn't realise it.

As my Europe trip was coming to an end, and I was due to return home and complete my honours, I received a call from my aunty asking if I had any work set up for when I arrived home. I didn't, and she was very happy about that. She was the prep teacher at an Orthodox Jewish school and needed a *teacher's aide* as she said, or a *slave* as my family said. She wanted me to work with her in the classroom and it led to very funny family discussions and opinions such as 'Jamie, you are just going to be her slave. I can't see it working out.' 'Why would you want to work in a school like that?' 'Will you guys manage, spending every afternoon together?' 'I can't see this lasting long, but give it a go if you want.'

For some reason I agreed to it, and it was the best decision I could have made. She spent hours on the phone with me, telling me what I could and couldn't wear and how I could and couldn't behave there. It is an extremely strict environment and a world that is very different from my own, but I knew I could respect it and manage if I wanted to. The first day of school came, and I met her friends and colleagues there. One of them said to me that I was so different to how she described me and that I was dressed completely appropriately. I wondered what she meant, of course I was, what did she think I was going to wear? I soon realised my aunty had painted me as this wayward wild child who runs around the world having fun, wearing no clothes, and had concerns about whether I could be managed or not.

I had the most fun year teaching a gorgeous group of prep boys how to read and write. We were the best team, and I loved being her slave. I didn't realise at the time, since it was the only classroom I had ever been in, but she was an incredible teacher – it comes as a natural talent to her. The class we taught had several students with significant needs, and her relaxed nature allowed those students to thrive. Who cares if he's sitting on a chair at the back of the mat and not the floor, she would say, as long as he is listening, it's all I need. I think our classroom looked like a wild jungle that year, and other strict teachers would be mortified, but to us it was perfect. She showed me how to account for lots of difficulties in students and, without knowing it, guided my entire career.

I absolutely loved working in that school and with children, and not long after starting I knew I was going to be a children's psychologist. It's funny how people are different – my aunt loves teaching a class and group of kids and doesn't enjoy one on one as much, whereas I never liked talking to the class but loved helping the individual students one on one. It was through her that I met my first psychology mentor and supervisor who I later ended up working for. And we still laugh about it, but I owe my entire career to my aunty, even if she was rude about the way I dressed and lived my life!

That school was the place where I learnt to be a psychologist and therapist, and for this reason it will always be a very special place to me. I was a teacher's aide there for two years, and in my placement year as a psychologist they allowed me to work there as a provisional psychologist under supervision. And then, as I graduated, they hired me as a real psychologist. When I share with people that I was the school psychologist there they are shocked for two reasons. Firstly, because they can't imagine me fitting in to the place. I strictly had to wear stockings, a skirt below my knees, and a shirt that covered my collar bones, and I had to tie my hair up. When I went to meet the head of the school with my hair down, he mentioned that my long hair walked into the room before I did.

Secondly, it was a community which had previously been somewhat reluctant to openly acknowledge mental-health difficulties. I don't know if psychology was accepted in the community or whether it was a taboo topic and coming from such a strong way of life and culture, I imagine it would have been hard for many families to find someone to connect to and be able to relate to. When people asked me, I say, 'Who am I to judge the way someone chooses to live their life? Yes, it is very different to my life, but I respect them and their choices, and that is how I am able to work as a psychologist there.'

And I was lucky to build beautiful relationships with the teachers, families and children I worked with throughout the six years I was there.

2020, the first year of lockdowns, was my last year at the school. I found the instability of schools opening and closing extremely unsettling and throughout the year the demand in private practice drastically increased. I was leaving school at 4 pm and going to see clients in my office at 4.30 or 5 pm and I wore myself out. I knew something had to give, and I knew it had to be the school. While it was the best place for me to begin my career, and a place I will never forget, I just lost the spark there. But I will always remember this school and experience fondly and be grateful for how it guided me to where I am today, even if I had to wear annoying clothes and did not have as much flexibility in my schedule as I do now.

CHAPTER 12

Psychology With Moshe

One thing that was important to me from the start was that I needed help with my personal life rather than my professional life. I know Moshe does lots of supervision of psychologists, and many young psychologists seek him out as a supervisor, but in my professional life I was already supported by the best teachers possible.

On some occasions, situations have arisen, and I've needed to debrief with Moshe, and again he has been very supportive in helping me understand what I have done, and how it may be useful. Moshe questions and questions me. 'Jamie, what did you say to them?' 'Jamie, how would you understand this?' 'Jamie, what were you doing there?'

And I will tell him, thinking I have probably done the wrong thing with my clients, and not knowing the language to use to describe what I had done. But somehow, he understands, and these conversations have taught me a lot.

Once I arrived at a session and announced I was having a mental breakdown and am really, really not good, with a big smile on my face.

*

Moshe Are you sleeping?

Jamie Yes, actually my sleep is better than it has been in ages.

Moshe Are you eating?

Jamie Yes, and quite healthily at the moment. I've had a good eating week.

Moshe Are you going to work?

Jamie Yes, I've had such a good work week. I've enjoyed myself this week.

Moshe Are you exercising?

Jamie Yes, I've been to gym three times this week, and gone on some walks.

Moshe Well Jamie, I hope that this is the worst mental breakdown you ever have in your life. We assess someone's level of distress by their functioning, and it seems like you are functioning very well at the moment.

*

I have remembered this ever since, and I now use it when necessary to understand my own clients' functioning. In one of our book meetings I had an important question to ask Moshe.

*

Jamie Moshe, in a book do you need to refer to the people you see as a clients or patients. In your book you refer to them as patients but let me read you what I wrote. I use a different word to you, but do you think it's OK?

You will notice throughout my writing that I have referred to the people I see as clients. It is a conversation Moshe and I have had several times, and we both feel the words clients and patients are not right - he even mentions it in the Foreword. He uses the word patients in his books, as does Lori Gottleib in her book, 'Maybe You Should Talk to Someone', but I could not. To me, the word patient implies that the person is sick, and I don't believe that is necessarily the case. I am more comfortable with the world client, even though there are difficulties with this word too. In my life, with my friends and family, I generally talk about 'the beautiful or cute children I spend my days with.' I see them all as little sparks of joy and believe my work is to help channel their energy in the right direction, whether they are a client or a patient.

Moshe Of course it is okay, because that is what you think and feel. Now you could quiz me more about my attitude. Number one, I think of you as Jamie – not my client or my patient. But in the English language we don't have another choice. Sometimes I refer to people like you as "the people I work with".

Jamie Yes exactly, but then they might think I was a colleague.

Moshe The categories that are available to us are clients or patients. I use the word patient because I started my work as a psychologist at Bouverie Clinic which was a child psychiatric clinic and the people there were referred to as patients. And when I become a family therapist in 1970, what happened was the person who was the reason for the referral was referred to as the IP, the identified patient. The theory behind the whole thing is that the family has the problem, and they identify someone as the patient. In that sense, I just accepted the tradition. But I have a problem with the word patient because it connotes sickness, which is what you are saying. On the other hand, it has certain advantages. The patient is also somebody who may have pain and hurt and it requires of the person who looks after them greater care, greater concern and greater *patience*. By contrast, the word client suggests, to me, as it suggests to the world, a commercial relationship. Usually, a purchaser is a client.

Jamie Yes, that is my difficulty with the word. It makes it seem transactional, and linked to money, but I have just never used the word patient, and I am not a clinical psychologist, but I have always used the word client. And not all the children I see are hurt or injured or sick. But do you think it is wrong if I call the people I see clients? I just couldn't use the word patient; it is just not me.

Moshe No, I don't think it is wrong. It is important and you need to use words you are comfortable with. There is always a problem in language. We often don't want to name things. But without naming you cannot communicate, and very often the language that is available does not do justice to what you are trying to communicate anyhow. I think, in some way, this is an important conversation for a different reason.

Part of being a good therapist, and a good human being, is to pay good attention to the language. I think we have a huge obligation, because words are like bullets. Sometimes they are more than bullets because bullets can be surgically removed, but hurtful words can stick with you for life. We also know the same word that is complimentary for you may be a painful word for someone else. To pay attention to the way we use language is very important.

*

"The limits of my language mean the limits of my world... Language shows us that naming an experience doesn't give the experience more power, it gives us the power of understanding and meaning."
—Brené Brown, *Atlas of the Heart*

In a more recent session, I explained to Moshe what had occurred earlier on in that day and asked him to help me with it. I explained that there was a little boy I worked with for years at school who might have been known as a naughty boy. He displayed violent outbursts and intimated his peers. We built a very strong rapport over the years and as he matured his behaviour significantly improved. I explained that I had seen him today for the first time since midway through the preceding year, and our session was mainly just connecting and catching up. Towards the end of the session,

I told him how proud I was of him for the way he is growing up so nicely. And then I turned my back to open the door for him and when I turned around again, he caught me off guard and gave me a hug, saying, 'Thanks, Jamie, can I please come again next week?'

*

Moshe   And you know what will happen now, you will be reported to the APS (Australian Psychological Society) for inappropriate conduct.

Jamie   That's why I haven't emailed anyone or documented it. I don't know what to do. You can tell me what to do!

Moshe   I can tell you already what I recommend you do. You enjoy the hug, Jamie.

Jamie   It was the most pure, beautiful thing that caught me completely off guard, and as he walked out, I thought to myself, Oh my goodness, what do I do, do I need to tell anyone about it?

Moshe   The APS has gone crazy, we are sick. By which I mean this. There are teachers and psychologists who are abusive and take advantage of and do terrible things to people, but sometimes the defence against it is as bad as the disease. If you talk to people, you will find they remember the teacher who was kind to them, or the teacher who spent time with them after school, etc., and nowadays those teachers are going to be reported.

*

Moshe went on to explain to me that this boy was trying

to thank me and show me that he appreciated what I had done for him through the hug. How could you possibly reprimand him for that?

*

Moshe What would the APS tell you to do?

Jamie I don't know, Moshe. Would I need to report it? What would I even report?

Moshe I'll tell you what I really think. This is such a crazy conversation. You are reporting a kid who hugged a woman old enough to be his mother. A child is saying thank you, I am grateful.

Jamie My heart was warm – it blew me away in the nicest way possible.

Moshe By the way I am happy for this to go into your book, and you can quote me, because by the time you publish the book, I will be too old… and you can go to jail or get kicked out of the APS… or blame me because I told you not to do anything about it.

*

In something I saw or read from Moshe, he described his experience of being a psychologist and I felt as if he had either taken the words out of my mouth or that I could have finished his sentences. Our thoughts about it are so similar and that made me smile. And Moshe's approach with me has helped me a lot with my approach to my clients. I am much more relaxed in sessions; I sit comfortably in my seat, and I don't take everything as seriously as I did before. I am much more *myself* as a practitioner and that has probably made me better at my job.

CHAPTER 13
Self Care

*

Jamie Moshe, I am going away soon.
Moshe That's nice, Jamie. Where are you going?
Jamie I'm going on my own for a few days to the coast and then meeting my three psychologist friends for a girls' trip.
Moshe Jamie, that is so nice, it is so important to be able to spend time on your own. I think it is something many people your age struggle with.
Jamie Yes, I love it. I never get bored – I think I was born in the wrong generation!
Moshe Well, there are endless things you can do these days, you can read, listen to music, look things up on the Internet. Many people your age struggled in lockdowns because they couldn't go to a night club, but in this day and age there are so many things one can spend their time doing.
Jamie Yes, I know, I always just have fun. I don't know what I do but I never get bored. The thing is, I kind of feel bad taking another week off because I just

had five weeks off over summer and haven't been back at work for too long and I'm not sure if it is fair to my clients. But I know I need to take more breaks this year and need to get away, so I am going.

Moshe What you are doing is taking care of yourself, and it is something that is so important. You have recognised that you need more breaks, and it is good you are taking one. How can a psychologist encourage other people to look after themselves if they don't know how to take care of themselves first?

*

This conversation made me feel so much better about my upcoming holiday. To me, self-care can be such an annoying cliché word, but it is very important. It is important to have things that make you feel nice and to do them, whether you are a psychologist or not. To me, it is not indulgent to sleep in if you need to sleep in, to take a day off work if you are run down or exhausted or to sit at home and get lost in a book or TV show for hours if that is what you need. I have become good at doing that and it makes my life much more enjoyable, even if my friends think I'm crazy… or lazy.

One form of self-care I have consistently done is yoga and I will never forget the first yoga class I went to. My best friend took me to a beautiful yoga studio and promised me it would be an easy class. This was just as I was recovering from glandular fever, and I felt like I needed to move my body. We got mats next to each other and about twenty minutes in, I was horrified that this was an 'easy' class. The room was boiling (27 degrees I think), I was sweating a lot and nothing about it felt easy. I started ranting to her during the class. 'What the hell, this isn't easy, why is the room so hot, I am sweating so much I swear I am going to kill you!' But, at the same time, I moved and opened my body in a way I never had before, and I knew I had to come back for more. And I did. In the next class the teacher asked me not speak during the class, and we all laughed when I told her I had been ranting about how hard it was for me. At the start of each yoga class I went to I would tell the teacher, 'I am very new, and I am not good at yoga, but I will just do what I can,' and that went on for years. To this day, I am still tempted to go up to the teacher at the start of each class and tell them I am not good and will do my best, but I can do it, and it doesn't matter if I am good or not. Real yogis are not watching what I am doing and are immersed in their own practice and breathwork.

In one class the teacher came and helped me get into a headstand, which I was able to hold on my own. *Me, Jamie, doing a headstand!* I was thrilled and also shocked that I could do it. I simply couldn't believe it! I went to her after and said, 'What the hell? How did you know I would be able to do that?' And she said she could see that I was ready to. Fast forward six years, and I have practised yoga consistently. I love everything about it. I have done classes in Melbourne, Byron, LA, Bali and India, and I booked a three-week Yoga Teacher Training for my thirtieth birthday. Another item on my bucket list. I don't want to be a yoga teacher, but I want the knowledge and to learn more about it. I am so grateful to my friend who took me to that first class, even though I'd threatened to kill her at the time!

Moshe and I ended up discussing the idea of vulnerability. I had sent him a list of dot points I wanted to discuss before the meeting. Here is a part of that conversation.

*

Moshe Jamie, there is something about the way we use language. You would not hesitate to tell me that you love chocolate ice cream. Or that you love Japanese food. But you couldn't tell me you loved L-word boy. I am putting it to you, what is that process? How do you understand that inability, reluctance, or fear of saying it? I know the answer.

Jamie Tell me.

Moshe In my view, you are scared of making yourself vulnerable.

Jamie Very much so, Moshe, and it's in my book.

Moshe And that's why I often don't tell you because you will work it out for yourself. And that is true of the way I have worked with you, meaning this. There are people whose hand you have to hold and walk them through because they cannot walk by themselves. And there are others who you just ask the question, give them a sense of direction and they can work it out. You are one of them.

Jamie Yes, it just takes a bit of time.

Moshe Yes, sometimes it is also important to give the person the time that they need.

Jamie Do you know Brené Brown?

Moshe Yes.

Jamie Well, when I went to India with my best friend years ago, she took one of her books, *Rising Strong*, with us which we both read and discussed in detail. Back then we laughed about how much we differed on the spectrum of vulnerability. She would meet someone and be in love five minutes later, whereas I would be hanging out with a guy and unable to admit I liked him after years. She wrote a letter about it to Brené Brown herself when we got back from the trip. Here is an extract from that letter:

> The concept of vulnerability (in a romantic context) became the theme of the trip quite quickly. There was this dance of contrasting levels of vulnerability between my best friend, Jamie, and myself. I wear my heart on my sleeve, I say exactly how I feel when I want to, I'm blunt, I don't play games, I thrive on intuition, I'm a hopeless romantic and love hard. Jamie is strong, cheeky, she's a professional teaser, she doesn't let boys in easily, she holds back her feelings until she knows the other side is committed, she's scared to feel feelings, yet she is the most virtuous and compassionate person I know.

Moshe Jamie, I want to ask you more about your India trip now, but it's not relevant. You asked me if I have ever had a real Savasana – how does that come into it?

*

He said this in a very confused tone, laughing.

*

Jamie   Yes, Moshe, have you ever had a real Savasana?

*

Savasana is the last part of a yoga class where you lie on the mat and allow all the movement and breathwork to integrate into your body. The English translation of Savasana is 'Corpse Pose,' and according to the Yoga Journal it is 'a meditative posture in which one lies on one's back, that is typically considered the final resting pose in yoga.' Savasana is a pose of total relaxation—making it one of the most challenging.

*

Moshe   Every time.
Jamie   Do you really, every time?!
Moshe   It depends on what you call real, you know. There is another family therapy book titled *How Real Is Real?* How do you judge real?
Jamie   You're lucky you get one every time.
Moshe   You know what Savasana means, by the way?
Jamie   Yes, it is in my book.
Moshe   Good. (He smiles and nods.)

*

The reason I wanted to know this is because I remember that in one session we had, Moshe asked me if *I* had ever had a real *Savasana*. The truth is, sometimes I have, and it is the most powerful and wonderful feeling. You let your mind go into a trance, with no thoughts, and there is no feeling like it. In my real Savasana, I feel energy radiating out of my skin into the universe throughout my whole body. At other times, however, I spend the entire Savasana fidgeting, thinking about work, where I am running to after yoga, what I will eat for breakfast, and so on.

*

Moshe At the end of yoga I've felt I have achieved a much deeper sense of relaxation. I have often thought at the end, after Savasana, was I in deep relaxation or was I actually asleep, and if I was asleep, was I cheating?

*

We both laughed.

*

Moshe And then I say to myself, what a stupid question! Who cares anyway? I'll tell you one more thing. There is one other phenomenon, and some people describe this big experience where you feel a sense of deep elevation, of euphoria, and I remember the first time it happened to me in my life.

*

Moshe told me about his experience and said that he doesn't usually like talking about it because it sounds like 'bullshit'. He said that generally, people who describe the experience of 'feeling at one with the universe' and 'everything feeling pure and blissful' can sound very silly. I then recited a quote from Iyengar to him: *Yoga is wisdom with innocence, not with arrogance.* I already knew that Moshe practises yoga every day, and now I know he has had real Savasana too. It is so impressive, and I certainly hope I am doing yoga every day at 83 years old. And I also hope my description of Savasana does not seem like 'bullshit'.

Moshe once emailed me a talk from ABC Radio National

between host Phillip Adams and Shannon Harvey, a journalist who spent a year meditating every day and had her brain monitored by scientists to determine if Mindfulness Meditation was worthwhile. The talk involved interesting discussion about mental-health difficulties, a lack of psychologists and psychiatrists in the world, and how Shannon found significant changes in her brain and her functioning following the experiment. She has written a book about it, *My Year of Living Mindfully*. She went on to complete a silent retreat which she trained very hard for, describing it as 'training for a mental marathon' and also as the 'best thing she had ever done in her life' besides marrying her husband and having her two children. While I don't think I am or ever will be fit for a silent retreat, my friends have often described me as a fairy and I am very grateful that I can have interesting conversations and learn from Moshe about this area too.

Recently I had a friend stay with me for some weeks. One night we were in my bed having a conversation about what we were each doing the following day. I told her I had an appointment with my naturopath, and how excited I was. She laughed at me and asked how many different people I see. I proudly told her I see Moshe for counselling, a naturopath, an energy healer, my GP, my professional supervisors and sometimes a numerologist who reads my birth chart.

'Jamie, it is just not normal to have so many people! it is so funny.'

'Oh, you don't understand. It takes an army to be Jamie – it's not an easy job!'

My wonderful naturopath has helped guide and support me with my physical health since I had glandular fever seven years ago. I see her as my doctor, someone who will be my doctor for the rest of my life, even if it is via natural remedies. She is an angel to me and has supported me just as much with my emotions too. Each time I see her, usually every few months, she puts me on her Vega machine, which, to most people would be absolutely woo-woo. According to the internet, Vega machines are a type of electro-acupuncture device used in Vega testing, which proponents claim can diagnose allergies and other illnesses.

According to me, it is a machine that knows more about me than I know about myself. I have had such crazy experiences with her and this machine that I just have to believe in it. I couldn't not.

I saw her about three months after getting back from India and told her I had become a vegetarian. At the time, it felt right for my body I explained to her. What I didn't tell her was that it has just been Passover and the night before Bobba had forced me to have a bowl of chicken soup. I didn't mind it as a one off and didn't even think about telling her. Anyway, she taps one end of the machine on my thumb and the other through her dials and on the base of the machine is this thing that screams out to her. Following the conversation, the machine started to make noises and ended up screaming and she said, 'Chicken, Jamie, chicken. Your body doesn't like it you're eating too much of it!' I almost fell off my chair and explained the chicken soup to her. I didn't mean to lie and I didn't think it was a big deal!

A few years later I became obsessed with Philadelphia cream cheese. It was so random; I hadn't eaten it in years. I was putting it on my toast, sometimes eating spoonsful of it plain (I know that is yuck) and really enjoying it. When I saw her at the following appointment, again the Vega machine started screaming. She looked at me and said, 'Cream cheese.' I told her how much of it I had been eating. The Vega machine also tells her my vitality and life/energy spirit at the time. When I was so sick with glandular fever, she told me I was like a 52-year-old. I knew, it's how I felt and how I acted. I wasn't surprised. And other times when I have been running around and living like a maniac, I will be 21 years old.

In other appointments, I have come to her saying I felt physically sick, and after using the Vega machine, she has explained to me it is actually my emotions that are making me sick and, annoyingly, she is always right. This machine even identifies the dates when things have occurred. She will ask me what happened seventeen days ago? And I will look through my phone and blab on about what had happened that day. It is the weirdest, scariest thing, that I enjoy so much. I say to people if you believe in it, it works, and if you don't there is no way it would ever work for you.

Funnily enough, a mantra she gave me to repeat to myself when I was facing a difficult time was, *I am open and ready to feel and heal.* To me, it is very important to take care of myself the best way I can, even if I have to see so many people. I believe Moshe would agree with this too, as part of the self-care that he recommends. Being able to discuss the holistic ways I look after myself with Moshe helps my therapeutic process, as it allows me to feel entirely understood by him. I know if he judged or did not take my fairy side seriously, I would be annoyed as it is all very important to me. What has been nice is that, through our discussions about yoga, holidays and self-care, I have come to learn that we generally do share a lot of the same views about these areas of life. Moshe is not fazed about me having so many people and encourages me to continually take the best care of myself I can.

CHAPTER 14
Hour 44

Following session 43, we decided I would write a book about my experience in therapy with Moshe, I continued to spent hours and hours writing. The words spilled out and I think it is one of the best things I have ever done. At first, I thought I would go to session 44 and read out what I had written to Moshe and then we could discuss it. But it didn't take me long, and in true Jamie style I had written about twenty pages in a week. I knew it wouldn't be possible for me to read that out in fifty minutes and have time to discuss it. I then thought about whether I should email it to Moshe or not. I just didn't know what to do. My gut feeling was that he wouldn't want to read it before the next session, but I emailed him just in case:

Hi Moshe – I hope you are having a nice week. I have written twenty-two pages of the book since last Friday and I think it is one of the most fun things I have done. Should I maybe send it to you before our session next week or just bring it in with me,
Kind regards, Jamie

Moshe replied: 'Delighted. Bring it along. Plus, a recording device if suits. See you then.' At our next session I walked into his office a couple of minutes early.

*

Jamie This session couldn't have come soon enough, Moshe, I have been so excited to see you.
Moshe And for me too, Jamie.

*

As I sat down, he could see the excitement spilling out of me and said something along the lines of I had to 'curb your enthusiasm'. My jaw dropped.

*

Jamie Excuse me, what did you just say?
Moshe I was playing with words and said 'curb your enthusiasm'.
Jamie Do you watch that show?
Moshe Yes.
Jamie I am about to faint. Moshe, you don't understand – I don't watch TV shows, but I have been watching *Curb Your Enthusiasm* since I was in isolation. Each night I watch an episode or two and it is the favourite part of my day. I laugh and laugh, and one of the chapters in the book is called "Small Talk to Medium Talk", a quote from Larry David!

*

Even Moshe looked a bit stunned and said it's meant to be. I went on to describe certain parts of my book to Moshe and explained how so many pieces of the therapy have come together for me through my writing. I used the anxiety example where I found the way he questioned me about areas in my life I had felt anxious about and then pieced it together right at the end so annoying. He said it was so good I could tell him that it was annoying. And in that one example I quoted, I may not have remembered the exact words he used correctly, but I remembered the sentiment correctly, and he believed it was deeply part of the way he wanted to work with people.

I explained to him that the only thing I wanted to do is write my book. How I have been working full time, keeping up a busy social life, trying to exercise, write psychology reports and somehow in between all of that I have found time to write and feel like it is giving me life.

*

Moshe Do you realise how lucky or fortunate you are? There are lots of people who write and want to write, but the actual writing is pushing shit uphill for them, whereas for you it is a joy, a release and an excitement.

Jamie This is the most honest I've ever been with myself; it is so good. All I can think about are ideas and chapters I want to write in my book. I am exhausting myself; my head doesn't stop flowing with ideas. I am such a nerd.

Moshe I think differently. You are lucky – enjoy it. And you know, it may mean something else.

Jamie What?

Moshe That you are a writer.

Jamie You know, maybe, I think I am, I actually think I

might be… I am quite proud of it, and it is making me feel so happy and empowered.

Moshe The way I understand it is that in somehow expressing it, even to yourself, you own the drama, the sadness of your life and it is very pleasurable and releasing. It is also turning unexpressed sadness into, hopefully, literature or poetry.

*

He went on to explain how in this book I am mastering the sad experiences in my life by turning them into writing, by using them as a psychologist to help other people and by making my own therapist happy. He could see I was finally allowing myself to be open and ready to feel and to heal.

*

Jamie I have had sessions that have been so hard for me, but we have still laughed – it hasn't been this manic way of you trying to fix me. You just sat there with me. You didn't try to change it.

Moshe I hopefully found a way of being gently humorous with you – that sounds like what you are saying to me.

> *"Your vision will become clear only when you can look into your own heart. Who looks outside, dreams, who looks inside awakens."*
> —Carl Jung (attributed)

Moshe then explained to me the importance of humour. How humour is an essence, it is our biggest friend, and that good humour helps you to cry and to be yourself. And that in the training of psychologists, they strongly warn you against humour, but from his point of view, in being human and being alive – we laugh. I then searched this entire document and realised in my most raw, personal pieces of writing about the most difficult parts of my life, the words laugh and laughed have been written thirty-eight times to this point. Even in difficult times there is always room for laughter, appropriately of course.

In 2015 Moshe ran a workshop for the Australian Psychological Society on 'Humour in Life and in Therapy', which I have watched on YouTube. In this talk Moshe mentions the advantages and disadvantages of humour both in life and in the profession of psychology. While he is 'pro' humour, he also points out how humour can be a form of cruelty or sadism.

'When used in the wrong way, it can be one of the most destructive, powerful tools amongst people to hurt and humiliate them and to put them down.'

In terms of working as a psychologist, Moshe mentioned the difference between laughing *with* or laughing *at*. 'When I laugh at, I fail, and when I laugh with, I succeed.' Moshe also explained in his talk that humour brings lightness, and that light is the opposite of black, the opposite of heavy. In general, life varies between dark and light, between heavy and light, or serious and humorous. As psychologists, if we want to encounter the whole of the person we are speaking to, we need to encounter both parts – we can't only pay attention to the dark side. We don't encounter the whole person unless we engage in the light side too.

In this talk he went on to share a joke he had told me in an earlier session, when I would have pretended to giggle. 'It is a common thing, for people who come to see me to feel awkward and unsure of how they are going, and to think of getting another opinion. I say to them I want to share a joke with you. And I tell them the following. "An Australian, a Frenchman and a Jew have been told the world is coming to an end in a week's time and they have one wish left. The Australian says he wants a free supply of beer and football every day. The Frenchman says he wants champagne and women, and the Jew says he wants a second opinion." I am therefore all in favour of second opinions and if you want one, don't feel bad about it. What am I doing here? I am making a point and saying I am comfortable with that, and don't feel tense, anxious, disloyal, or guilty – if you are not sure, feel free. I don't always do it, but hopefully when it is appropriate, I do.'

Moshe continued to explain that one of the most powerful experiences of intimacy is the capacity to engage in humour, and that humour doesn't need to be hilarity, it can simply bring a gentle smile to your face. When Moshe asked me about how I spent time with L-Word boy, amongst other things I told him that we laughed a lot together – about me, about him and about life in general. This must have been when Moshe realised the degree of our connection as he told me laughing is one of the most important forms of intimacy. I didn't know that before.

In therapy and in life, you can use humour to avoid talking

about different subjects and you can use humour as a way of making it possible to talk.

'Those who don't understand that it can be used both ways don't, I think, understand the way life works,' Moshe said.

On reflection, Moshe and I have used both forms of humour in my therapy. It works so well for me and my personality, and I wouldn't have been able to get to where I have without his gentle and compassionate humour.

Towards the end of hour 44, it was critical for me to tell Moshe that I had quoted him, using his words and his learning throughout the book, and I thought it was important for him to read it and check that he was comfortable with everything. Here is how the conversation went.

*

Jamie I have written this book from my perception of the things you have tried to tell me. But you know two people can see the same event occur and have completely different accounts of it… Are you going to read it?

Moshe Just at this point, I don't want to read it.

Jamie Oh my G-d.

Moshe I'll tell you why… What you have told me is that you are on a roll, I don't want to spoil your thing. I would rather do what we are doing… talk about it, discuss it… I like the fact you are recording this session and the way it feels now – it feels so comfortable. Keep it away from me.

Jamie But one day you have to read it, by the way.

Moshe I will read it after it gets published… I don't know.

Jamie But I have quoted you, and spoken about lots of things you have said, and if I have misunderstood or misrepresented you, it is your right to tell me or let me know. I won't be upset or annoyed. I promise!

Moshe The only thing I would say to you at this point… if you quoted me, and you are concerned that you have misquoted me, check with me. What you are writing is the way you remembered it, and if you remember it differently to the way I said it, what difference does it make? I am not worried if you have said terrible things that will get me into court, I don't care. Basically, we are on the same wavelength, and if you remember it differently from the way I said it, so what? You are telling your life, through our sessions. It's about you, how you remember and what you have made of our sessions. I have done the reverse for many years, I have written about many people and tried to do it the best I could, but I know that is the way I remember what they have said to me.

*

I then asked Moshe to sign two of his own books, *Corrupting the Young* and *The Answer Within*, which I had never read but wanted to take with me on my upcoming holiday. His response was, 'And what's wrong with my third, book *Resilience?*'

*

Jamie Moshe, I already have that one. I loved it and I have actually given it to so many other people to read.

*

He signed the books for me.

To Jamie, My co-author. In friendship, Moshe

And then told me that he doesn't care about his own books and is much more excited about mine.

CHAPTER 15

Friends

When Moshe signed the book and wrote 'In friendship,' it made me feel happy. While I didn't exactly consider him one of my friends, he is. He is someone I greatly admire and enjoy speaking to, even if I am paying him. In fact, it wasn't only my mum who said my face lights up when I speak about him, but my friends have noticed it too. One friend once asked me to give him Moshe's number for his own therapy.

'Why do you need to go to my psychologist? Go find your own psychologist!'

'Well, Jamie, you have just raved about him for the last three years!'

'Okay, I will send his number. I'm joking about him being my psychologist only, and I think anyone that gets to see him is extremely lucky.'

That friend also went on to ask me if I thought Moshe thought about me out of our sessions.

'Absolutely not!' I responded. 'He has his own life. He gives me his undivided attention during our sessions, but I really don't think he thinks about me much in between them.'

Not only as a client but as a psychologist, you need to learn to have *thick skin*. We are people too, with empathy and extreme care for our clients (hopefully). However, we are all entitled to live our own lives.

'How do you not take it home with you?' I am often asked about my work. The truth is I do, of course I do. Sometimes I have sessions in which I want to cry and feel so sad afterwards. And sometimes I have sessions where I am very confused and feel as if I still have absolutely no idea what I am doing as a psychologist. At other times I am so proud I can't wait to share what has happened in supervision. However, most of the time, I now finish my workdays and enter my own life where I am Jamie, just a person, just like the children, teenagers, parents and teachers I spend my days talking to.

One quote that has stood out to me for several years is this: The circles of women around us weave invisible nets of love that carry us when we're weak and sing with us when we're strong. It is written by SARK (Susan Ariel Rainbow Kennedy), one of my mum's favourite authors, in her book, *Succulent Wild Woman*. It is a strong message Mum has always taught me – Jamie, your girls are so important, it is so important to have strong friendships as they will hopefully be everlasting and support you through the good and the bad that life brings. Boys will come and go but your friends will be the ones that are always by your side.

I am so very lucky to have the most beautiful circle of women in my life who are all close to my heart. In fact, as I write this, I have realised it is not only women, but men (as Moshe would say) or boys (as I would say) too. Since I moved from Auckland, I have managed to make friendships that feel like they will last a lifetime. I am busy writing this paragraph as I am sitting in my high-school bestie's house. We haven't lived in the same city since school but have the same closeness more than ten years later. When I told him I was coming to Queensland, he said, 'I will not have you stay at any other place than my house,' to which I said, 'Okay, I believe you. You know I'm not the type of person to really ask for things, but I am comfortable to stay in your house and am so excited too, thank you.'

My friends and I have supported each other in our careers and job progressions, through flings and break ups, had amazing holidays together and laughed and cried together in sickness and in health. I have also managed to uphold two close friendships from when I was living in New Zealand fourteen years ago. One curse of COVID for me was that I have not been able to see them for years now and I'm counting the days until we can catch up in real life.

One of the best books I have recently read is *The Happiest Man on Earth* by Eddie Jaku. You will have already noticed his quotes throughout my writing. Eddie is a Holocaust survivor who survived concentration camps – the most difficult of circumstances and experiences I could not even begin to fathom. It is a miracle he survived, and he believes part of his survival was due to the very strong friendship he shared with his friend, Kurt Hirschfeld. Eddie writes that at the start of each day in Auschwitz he and Kurt would meet up and walk and talk in order to keep their spirits alive. If one was lucky enough to receive extra food, they would save some for the other, and vice versa. Eddie writes that they 'were able to look after each other' and that is real friendship. He writes in his book: 'That is the most important thing I have ever learned: the greatest thing you will ever do is be loved by another person. I cannot emphasise this enough, especially to young people. Without friendship, a human being is lost. A friend is someone who reminds you to feel alive.'

Research shows that social connections are an important pillar of happiness. I learnt about this in a course I completed through Yale University soon after we entered lockdown, 'The Science of Wellbeing' by Laurie Santos. It is one of the most popular courses at Yale and can be done for free online. What stood out to me is that what we think makes us happy is not what actually does. Rather than buying nice things, being married, making lots of money, it is savouring moments we enjoy, being socially connected, finding gratitude, sleeping well, exercising and doing things for other people with nothing in return. Laurie explains that being around other people matters more than we think it does. Very happy people have more social connections and strong family ties, and those qualities are important for physical and mental health. Maybe that is why I have been able to feel happy a lot of my life – the social connections I have are strong, reciprocal and, most of the time, thoroughly enjoyable.

A special group of friends I have are my psychologist friends. We have upheld and created a beautiful friendship group. We all work in different areas of psychology and meet for dinners and wines to discuss our work and our personal lives. We always seem to be that loud, annoying table, screaming and crying with laughter, while other diners look at us and think 'Shut up!' After one of my trips to America, I told these friends a story which they have forced me to include in this book! When I told them this story their jaws dropped and, like my Uni friends, they could not believe that I had such a wild side. The following is that story.

Another item on my bucket list, besides writing a book and completing yoga teacher training, was to attend the Coachella Music Festival in California. I woke up in the middle of the night with my best friend to book tickets for Coachella. I had just finished my placement year and was finally registering as a real psychologist after six years. As the time came closer, I realised that I didn't want to go on the trip. I wanted to save money and start my career. I took this friend out for a Japanese dinner to tell her. The joke was, she didn't listen to me and told another friend of ours she knew I would end up coming. I didn't know how to make it clearer to her. Telling her to find someone else to go with and to SELL MY TICKET. Luckily enough, she didn't listen to me. Apparently, she knew intuitively that we would end up going together.

One day, towards the end of the year I learned that I had failed two case studies which I needed to pass in order to become a registered psychologist. I had never failed anything in my life. On top of that I did not get the dream job I had wanted to begin the following year. What a day! I know I definitely ate lots of chocolate and called my friend to tell her we were definitely going, and she laughed. 'I told you so.'

Off we went, running around Vegas, LA and then to Palm Springs for the festival. In Vegas, we met some men who put us in touch with their friends who would be at Coachella. On our second day we texted them, and they told us they were chilling at someone's house, and we should go. Not knowing them, we decided it was best to stay at the festival and we went on enjoying our day. We stayed in touch with them and later learnt the house they had been *chilling* at was Post Malone's. HOW DUMB WERE WE? How did we not go with them, we thought? So, we decided that if they messaged us the following day, we would leave the festival to meet them no matter what.

The end of the third day arrived, to our surprise they stayed in touch with us. They told us they were going to another party that night and that we couldn't Uber there but that they would meet us somewhere in the area and pick us up. 'We're going,' said my friend. I agreed, although I felt a bit scared. We ended up Ubering to a random petrol station in the middle of nowhere, ran inside and bought deodorant, face wipes and mints to try to freshen up and waited to be picked up by. I was very nervous and thought this is exactly what your parents tell you not to do.

Minutes later two men arrived in a very fancy Rolls Royce and one of them was Jewish, which immediately made us feel somewhat connected. We drove into an estate and down a two kilometres driveway to a house that overlooked the entire festival. Everyone there was a someone and being from Australia seemed to be cool enough for us to be there too.

That night was one I will never forget in my entire life. It was a party like in the movies. We were so out of our league but having an absolute ball, and somehow fitting in well enough. We made it back to our place by 7 am. My friend stopped off at The Parker, Palm Springs, for breakfast on the way home. I went back to sleep. I don't have many photos or videos of that night, but I can picture every detail, from the mansion to the food, to the people and the view of the wonderful festival. It was at that party that, for the last time ever, I made the mistake of telling someone I was a psychologist and not a fashion designer. He immediately sat down with me on a couch for an hour or two, telling me his life story, while I sat there thinking to myself, how do I shut him up without being rude or seeming uncaring?

These were some of the responses my psychologist friends said at the dinner following this story (and they still remind me of it often): 'Your life is a joke, Jamie.' 'How do these things happen to you?' 'Jamie, I am shocked! How could you be so reckless! 'I didn't know you had this side to you! Who are you?'

People around me often tell me that I am a very lucky person. Lucky things happen to me. And happen often. And I agree to an extent. I told Moshe my perspective on this as we were talking about how well our matching had gone and discussing psychology in general.

*

Moshe In all of it there is a certain degree of luck. There is a sense of randomness in science, and unpredictability. And so far, we have been lucky.

Jamie I think in lots of ways you create your own luck. I get told often that I am a lucky person. And I am, I believe I am. But I have done things that have given me the luckiness. I chase after what I want and often am lucky to get it, but I've also worked hard for it. I left you the note because I didn't think I'd be able to speak to you. And overall, Moshe, honestly, in my life what I have experienced is the *harder* I work, the *luckier* I get.

Moshe If you try your luck, you will be lucky sometimes, but if you don't you definitely won't.

*

As I am a 'deeply emotional person', when I feel excited about something it is all I can talk about. Whether it is a new crush, an upcoming holiday, a new pair of shoes or my birthday party. Once I had decided I was writing the book with Moshe I went around telling all of my friends. One of my older and wiser friends said to me, 'Jamie, what's wrong with you? Stop telling everyone until you know you're actually doing it.' I agreed – he was right – but basically, I couldn't help myself. I have been overwhelmed by all of my friends' support in writing this book and the fact that they all wanted to read it. Most of them, if not all, have actually read it now. When I've spoken about it with them, they've all said they hope they are in it. I've asked why would they want to be in my book and that if they are it means I'm talking about them in therapy, so they shouldn't actually want to be in it!

As with my work, my friendship life is quite amazing and not something I often need to talk about with Moshe. When I do find myself in annoying situations on the odd occasion, I bring them up with him. And guess what, he does what he always does, encourages me to communicate openly and honestly with them too. Moshe teaches me to stand up for myself and explains that if my friends can't understand that then I need to think about whether they are worth being friends with or not.

At one point I spoke in depth about a situation that had occurred with Moshe where I really found his stance helpful. At the end, he said to me, 'Jamie I can't wait to read about this chapter in the book.' And Moshe, my answer for you is, this is that chapter.

CHAPTER 16
Wedding Season

'Oh, my goodness, Mum, I think I'm at the age now where people get married!'
'Yes, my darling. Have you only just noticed?'

I mentioned earlier in the book a very difficult time for me. And as it so happened around that time I had an engagement party to attend every single weekend. I was in such a vulnerable state, feeling extremely sad and insecure and somehow, I had to be happy for all of my friends. And the truth is, I was happy for all of those friends but, in that month, it felt so very hard. I was broken. My family kept telling me to tell Moshe to 'up his game' or that I needed to find a new psychologist. I knew my feelings had nothing to do with the therapy Moshe was or wasn't providing, and in fact am very grateful for the way he supported me then.

No one could have done anything about how I was feeling, and at some stages I became concerned that I would never get out of it. These were, by far, the most difficult *growing pains* I have experienced. But like everything in life, with time, patience, anxiety and tears, they subsided.

I remember finally telling Moshe, 'I'm not there yet, but I am slowly starting to feel a tiny bit like Jamie again.' It was my birthday night that helped me change my mindset. I didn't want to celebrate it at all (which is very unlike me) – I just wasn't in the mood. I think I was freaking out about turning over another year and being single, a feeling I had never experienced before.

*

Jamie Moshe, oh my G-d, I am just so old, I'm not coping.
Moshe Jamie, look who you are saying that to. How can you tell someone like me you are old? (He laughed.)
Jamie Sorry, I know you are actually old, but I feel like I am too in a different type of way, you know.

*

I remember having the same conversation with a colleague at work. She understood my situation and my anxiety well but questioned me too.

'Jamie, think about how much life you've lived. Would you want your life to be any other way?'

The answer to that question was no. I feel as if I have had the most amazing life with the best and most fun experiences, and while I was deep down so happy for all of my friend's engagements, not one part of me had ever wished it was me with a ring on my finger. Even if I was having a mental breakdown at the time they all got engaged.

My birthday night ended up being one of those amazing, fun, unexpected nights – no surprise there, since I was dreading it so much. It's always the functions you don't want to go to that are the most fun and the nights you plan and are excited for that are sometimes a letdown. We weren't in lockdown but had to make bookings to go to places and plan and be prepared – something I don't like and am not good at doing in my social life. I had tentatively booked a restaurant for eighteen people weeks before, but didn't do anything about it. It got to the point where my friends started texting me in the days before. 'What are we doing for your birthday?' 'You really need to organise it and let people know because otherwise we will make other plans.' 'Jamie, just do the dinner – come on, it will be so much fun.'

I am so happy that I gave in and listened to my friends. We had a delicious dinner, went to a bar afterwards and all ended up at my apartment. It was a wild and fun night. Two boys that night tried to kiss me. I remember thinking maybe I still had it after all! For some reason I really needed that night with my friends – having fun, laughing and being reminded how loved I am, after a period when, for the first time in my entire life, I had felt lonely.

Soon after that night we ended up in another dreaded lockdown, during which I continued to re-build myself and again got to the point where I was living my best life. I was finally Jamie again, happy, bubbly Jamie, at the beach every day, doing telehealth at home and socialising where and when it was appropriate.

Fast forward eight months and all the engagements turned into weddings – I was invited to five weddings in an eight-week period. And being Jewish weddings, they were all on Sundays. I became an expert at weddings and knew exactly what I would do if married one day. I have noted the different types of venues, cocktails, foods, times of the day and I've even made friends with the wedding photographers who joked I go to almost as many weddings as they did.

I remember going for a walk with my mum before the weddings started and she asked me how I felt about attending them on my own. I told her I was feeling fine about it for some reason and explained to her that I am more used to being on my own than being with a partner.

At two of the weddings, I have felt my eyes tear up during the Chuppah ceremony, my favourite part of weddings. The Chuppah is the most spiritual part where two souls become one. I enjoyed each one and, in some cases, more than I thought I would. Not once did I feel insecure about being single at them, despite occasionally being questioned by different adults there. 'So, who do you belong to? 'Myself,' I would answer. Or 'Shame, it is very hard being single at your age, isn't it?' 'Maybe for some people it is,' I would say, 'but much to my grandparents dismay I am actually very happy at the moment and don't find it hard at all.'

This might sound vain, but one thing that has helped me survive the wedding season is that I felt nice in what I was wearing at each one. Shopping and preparing my outfits cost me an arm and a leg but it was so worth it. Before each wedding I organised my amazing hairdresser to come and do my hair and she acted as a buffer between my sessions with Moshe. As she curled my hair we would talk and laugh about the gossip of each wedding, which boys I was excited to see there and which boys I wanted to avoid. I planned and prepared what I would wear and somehow managed to have the best two months ever. It was so fun to celebrate and be part of such a special day with the very special people around me and my heart felt so full with the love overflowing at these events.

I have told this to Moshe too, when he, as Mum had, asked me, 'How did you feel at the weddings on your own, Jamie?'

*

Jamie You know, I have been fine. They have been so much fun. And it is so strange, but for some reason, at the moment, I have even felt proud of myself.

Moshe Even?

Jamie Yes. Why are you querying that word?

Moshe Because it suggests that you think that there is something wrong with being proud of yourself. You should be proud of yourself and there is nothing wrong with that.

Jamie Okay, I am proud of myself. Is that better?

*

One of my cheeky friends, who reminds me of Larry David, made a joke about the upcoming wedding season. 'How many of the five couples do you think will end up getting divorced?' My heart dropped and I got a horrible feeling in my tummy. I replied, hopefully none. Why would they even ask such a thing. And then I thought, well, this is how is starts out, we don't know how it is going to end. No one does.

CHAPTER 17
Hour 45

*

Moshe Is my receptionist still downstairs?
Jamie She is leaving now, and she asked me to tell you that she will speak to you on Friday.
Moshe And you are the messenger again?
Jamie I am the messenger and remember, last time my message was that he was going to lock up.
Moshe And you could refuse to be the messenger and say talk to him yourself.
Jamie I don't mind being the messenger. How are you, Moshe? Are you good?
Moshe I am good but, by the way, as someone who has acquired English formally, it is well, not good.
Jamie Moshe, are you well? I have never used formal language, and my friends have always teased me that English is my second language.

*

Then, for some reason, I asked Moshe if he thought in English or in Hebrew, and we had a discussion about this. He said it depended on the topic. For example, when he thinks of his time in the Israeli army he thinks in Hebrew, but if he thinks about studying psychophysics at university, he thinks in English. I told him I didn't even know what psychophysics was, and he explained it was a second-year psychology subject he had studied. I told him I was so bad at science; I once told my science tutor a natural disaster in the Kruger National Park may be a tsunami.

*

Moshe Jamie, I am dying to ask you, how is your writing going?

Jamie Oh, my G-d, it is so good! I have just been away for a weekend alone and I actually had time to figure out my book. The one afternoon was raining and I just sat and wrote and wrote and wrote.

Moshe So you were in a zone, you were flowing.

Jamie My whole book came together. I was writing and writing, and I sort of had no idea but thought I should put some order into it. Well, no, it was written in order, but I didn't know where the end was or the way it would all be, but now I do. It is twenty chapters so far and I have written nineteen of them.

*

Moshe's eyes widened at that, but he didn't say anything.

*

Jamie I know I am a nut job.

Moshe By the way, that is not what I said, that is what you said.

Jamie Moshe, you have so much stuff. So many articles,

podcasts, books. It might sound weird, but I am stalking you. There are so many things I want to read and add into my book. I have already written one part, about how you described your experience of being a psychologist, and as I wrote that it was so weird because either I could have finished your sentences, or you could have taken the words out of my mouth. Well, I found that interview, and I plan on re-watching it and adding more detail in my book. I knew it wasn't in a session we had, or your school talk or in your book *Resilience*, but I knew I had seen it somewhere and I was so excited when I found it. Your six-part video about the joy of therapy.

Moshe You know what I like best, it's when you say you don't know if I pinched your words or if you pinched my words. I had a professional partner; he worked next door to me and we wrote a lot together. Before we started writing together, we had lunch every day, and over the years we would argue with each other – "No, I told *you* that." 'No, you told *me* that." It reminds me of that.

Jamie Moshe, I need to sort out my life a bit. I need to work. I have psychology reports to write, and I might be doing a talk for a school next week, and that takes time, and I have to balance my book and my life. There's a lot of good stuff going on, but a lot.

Moshe By any normative standard if, after the few weeks

we are talking about, you have got twenty chapters or nineteen chapters, you have a book there. You are in a flow; you are in a zone. If it takes a bit longer it doesn't matter. I know that when you are in a thing like that it is all you want to do and everything else is an interference.

Jamie Yes, everything, my entire life, is interfering with my book. All I want is to be alone in peace and quiet and write my book! Anyway, we could spend the whole session discussing it, but I have a few life things to discuss too.

*

I went on to talk about some things that led us into a discussion about the statistics of infidelity in marriages. The statistics show that 30 per cent of wives cheat on their husbands and 50 per cent of husbands cheat on their wives. Moshe had previously told me this in a much earlier session and I couldn't understand why. In fact, I was mad at him for telling me these numbers. But in that session, he went on to explain that in all the marriages that split up, the interesting thing is that most of the divorcees do not regret their marriage and that many go on to get remarried and are okay. I knew my parents were happy when they married and they love me and my brother and I don't think they regretted it either. In fact, I know they don't. Moshe bought it up again in this session.

*

Jamie Yes, you've told me about the numbers before and I don't want to hear them again. I am trying to see marriage as a nice thing and when you tell me those numbers, I think why does anyone do it?

Moshe My job is to make you face reality. (He laughed.)

Jamie See, Moshe, maybe I'm not so dumb after all.

Moshe I'll say it another way too. There is lots of cheating going on, lots of extramarital affairs, but it's not always cheating because there are some people who are open about it and okay with it.

*

In his book *Resilience*, Moshe writes in his reflection on the 'Couples' section, 'Language is our tool of communication, but what is meant cannot be taken for granted; the meaning often needs to be explained. Extramarital relationships are described as "adultery", "mortal sin" or "betrayal" by some, while others call them "playing around", "a bit on the side" or "swinging". The different language indicates the conflicting attitudes prevalent in our society.

*

Moshe So, you have been writing in the book about the L word and stuff?

Jamie Yes. (I rambled on for ages about an annoying situation I found myself months or, embarrassingly, years later.)

Moshe Writing the book, has it had an effect on how you think and feel about him?

Jamie Yes, definitely. Writing my book has helped me realise I need to end it with him. I believe in myself more. I was so insecure and not confident most of my life, even though I come across to people so differently. I am more secure in myself and in who I am now, and I might even think a guy is lucky if I like him. I don't know why, but I have so much more belief in myself. I don't have the space, time or energy to chase after someone who isn't going to give me the time or attention I need. I think I might tell him I L him and *dump* him in the same conversation… if he makes time to see me.

*

We both cracked up laughing.

*

Moshe Jamie, you know the truth can set you free! And one other thing I want to say – I wish in a way that you had recorded our previous sessions. I will tell you what you would notice – that the sound of your voice is different today to the way it was a few weeks ago.

Jamie Why?

Moshe You sound much more definite, confident, different, and flowing too…

Jamie Really? (I interrupted him loudly.)

Moshe You are just flowing, saying what is on your mind.

Jamie Well, that is everything you have taught me.

Moshe So, it's all my fault?

Jamie Yes. It's interesting that you can notice my voice sounds different. All you ever do is tell me to communicate honestly and openly. Well, it's not all you do, but it is basically in every chapter. Moshe, the book is the best thing ever, everyone should just write a book.

Moshe Writing is obviously part of who you are. That is not me, it's not the therapy – you may have known all along, but now you are doing it, it feels free and natural, and it works for you.

Jamie You know, every time I have gone away, I have taken a journal. I have added stuff from those journals from years ago into my book. If I go to a conference, these days it is all PowerPoint slides, but that doesn't do it for me. I always take an exercise book and write my notes out and keep them. I also have all my supervision notes from when I was learning to be a psychologist, and sometimes when I find the notebook I read over them. It is still great learning for me.

Moshe What's the earliest writing you have that you've done?

Jamie I would shudder to read it, but it was a year after I finished school, a journal I took away with me when I travelled to Thailand, Laos and Cambodia when I was nineteen. I found it the other day. I've included some excerpts in my book of writing I've done on my travels – maybe I have always enjoyed writing, you know.

Moshe Tell me this, in your writing – it started with the COVID business – how much of that have you done?

Jamie A bit, but it's kind of all the way through it. Do you want to know the chapter names?

Moshe No, keep telling me about COVID for now.

Jamie The one chapter is mainly on your talk about COVID at the school – and then throughout lots of the other parts I just reference it, like lockdowns and stuff.

Moshe I want to tell you something. When I was thinking about the COVID part, I gave two talks on the pandemic. One is the one you know, and the other one I gave in Hebrew. I then decided I would get it translated for you (I shriek in the background), but I got buggered up in the technology of it. It is recorded on something that is to do with Facebook. I want to make the talk available to you, as I said lots of stuff I didn't say in my school talk.

Jamie Yes I would love that.

Moshe There are a few options. One option is you get it in Hebrew and find someone to translate it for you, and then you can listen to it. If that is difficult somehow, if you find a way, which I don't know because I am stupid at these things, to transfer it so that I can listen to it in Hebrew, and I won't do it in the sessions with you because that's an independent thing, but we will meet and I will listen to it, tell you and then go beyond and have a conversation about it.

Jamie Please can we do that?

Moshe Yes, but you need to deal with the technology for me in the first place. At this point I buy out, and it is between you and my assistant.

Jamie   Moshe, my brother already thinks I'm too obsessed with you, and I put that in my book, but this would just be amazing! I am so excited! I talk about you a bit outside of here, but I promise not that much.

Moshe   And I haven't even paid you to advertise me.

Jamie   Moshe, you are so clever. I loved all the things you said to the parents of your school talk, and so many of your messages were so special. I think they can maybe help people, simple messages that are so important. I would love to translate this with you together and add it if you are happy to and don't mind spending your time doing that.

Moshe   I made you an offer. I am happy to do it.

Jamie   Yes, that would be better than me finding someone else to translate it.

Moshe   Yes, and then the headache can be all yours to do what you want with it.

Jamie   It is not a headache. The only headache right now is me trying to live my life and function like a person while managing this writing.

Moshe   Well, we have both discovered that you are a writer.

Jamie   What if you read it and change your mind?

Moshe   Jamie, I don't know if you are a good writer or a bad writer – it is not about that. But you experience joy in writing and the flow, and you are telling me people in your life so far have appreciated it and responded to it. In writing, there are people who speak languages differently, but the key thing for all writers is to find their own voice. Some people write but you can hear or read they are writing in someone else's voice. It is clear that if you are in a flow, you are speaking in your own voice. And you know what, after speaking to you today I am even happier in my decision not to read it at this stage.

*

I was hoping he would be telling me the opposite as I was really bursting for him to read it.

*

Jamie   But Moshe, you just have to read it. I don't know if I will be able to manage much longer, but we can discuss it at the next session.

*

CHAPTER 18

Lessons From Covid

I had finished my consulting work early and was very excited about having a free afternoon to do whatever I liked. I had planned to get my nails done, maybe go for a walk or to a yin yoga class and to write some work reports.

Every second Wednesday afternoon I am free, and I love it. On the alternating day I consult, see Moshe at 5 pm and come home for a team meeting from 6.30 to 8 pm. As I was leaving, I called Moshe's receptionist to check in and see what was going on with Moshe's Hebrew video on COVID. She explained to me that she was waiting for Moshe to call her and arrange his day and would get back to me shortly. Twenty minutes later she called me and told me that Moshe would call me at 5 pm. 'Perfect,' I said.

When Moshe called, he explained that he knew what he said in his video and instead of translating it, he suggested we should rather do more of an 'interview' about COVID. I could ask him any questions I wanted and could 'use him as much as possible'. I was even happier with this. We proceeded to have an hour-long phone conversation, which I recorded about the pandemic and what it has done to the world and the people in it. Together we decided Moshe would start talking to me and as we went along, I could ask him questions. I noticed throughout this conversation that his voice sounded different from the way it does in our sessions. He sounded more formal, like a teacher, somehow even wiser than usual. I thoroughly enjoyed him sharing these ideas.

He began by saying, 'In my more jocular way, I have argued that the corona virus was invented or designed by psychologists to get more business, and they are joint in this with dog breeders and bread shop owners.'

*

Moshe Psychologists have become as busy as you can imagine and my problem with psychologists is that they emphasised and promoted the dangers and the problems of COVID. What they have not illuminated, promoted or talked about is the other side of it. Any human crisis is also a human opportunity. In every area of life, that has been recognised. The Buddhists say that emptiness is untold possibilities. And in Judaism there is a saying (which he recited in Hebrew) – 'from nothingness my help would come' – nothingness will be the source of your help. And psychology, in all of its public announcements, has never highlighted that aspect. It is very good for business, but it is not good for the health of the nation, in my view.

Jamie So, psychology doesn't realise that something like this can be powerful or can be an opportunity to grow. Is that what you are trying to say?

Moshe I am not trying to say it, I *am* saying it. I am saying that crisis is an opportunity, pain is also the pain of growing. (I giggled in the background, knowing how much I have referred to growing pains in this book.) Growth is about pain, crisis and difficulties, and what is most talked about are the dangers and not the opportunities. To be clear, I am not saying there are no dangers, there are serious dangers, and there have been people who have suffered untold pain because of it. People have died because of the virus and people have died alone without their loved ones around them. But I think what is important is to also enumerate and highlight and describe the opportunities and the examples of people benefitting from it, and it is terribly important to tell people that they can benefit from it too.

Jamie Moshe, in your work over the last two years, what are the benefits and opportunities you have seen? Are you willing to share any, or is that too personal?

Moshe There is one story that stood out to me. A man who had been seeing me for a number of years. His mother was in an old people's home, and he was told her days were numbered, and he felt terrible about the possibility he would not be with his mother. He struggled with this, talked to me about it and made the decision to take her home. He took her home, and the nursing home made him sign every document and he found the inner strength, signed away and nursed her to her death. His own worth, confidence, and pride that he was able to refuse to accept society's dictates and carve his own place, and do it his own way, was an incredible experience for him in gaining additional self-respect and self-esteem. Bringing his mother home brought about huge changes in his life, and he made COVID an opportunity for growth and development. You know what he is doing now, Jamie? He is doing a counselling course; he is going to set up in competition with you and me.

Jamie Good Moshe, we need him. (I said, laughing.)

Moshe And this is just one example of many. The common one is parents and children being thrown together and families spending much more time together. Or new Dads who were able to spend the first two years of life with their children too, because they were working from home. Some Dads I have spoken to are delighted with this. They have been able to take on a much bigger role in raising their children. Let me talk about myself. For two years I have worked from home on and off, and while I hate it, it gave me a chance to cook, clean and sometimes talk to you on the phone and lie down if I wanted to.

Jamie How nice is that!

Moshe To describe it all as a tragedy is tragic. I remember telling the story of Newton, who was in isolation for two years during the black plague, and it is then that he discovered the laws of gravity, etc. And also, the number of people who have written novels during the COVID period.

*

I started laughing, of course I start writing a book *after* the lockdowns.

*

Moshe You see, COVID has helped you learn that you are too slow.

Jamie I never do things the way they are meant to be done. Writing is a perfect lockdown activity, and it is so typical of me to write a book as soon as lockdown ends!

Moshe No, you are doing it when lockdown is coming towards the end. There may still be lockdowns – we don't know. Also, COVID has given you the material to write about. In truth, it has been the stimulus for you to ask me if we can write about it.

Jamie And this interview isn't about me, and I don't want to get into it too much, but more than that, it has been the biggest blessing in my world and my life.

Moshe Tell me how.

Jamie Well I have written how, but you refuse to read it, so I will tell you. I came to you just before COVID, thank G-d, but it has given me the time I needed to process what I needed to process, and to work through big things in my life. I can't remember the words you just said but having everything stripped gave me time to be with myself. I had time to be sad when I needed to be sad and work through what I needed to. I have needed a lot of time, and all of that time has helped me to get to where I am now.

Moshe I quoted it today. One of the first things I said to you today was to quote the Zen Buddhist saying, 'emptiness is untold possibilities'. And that is what I just heard you saying. And there is no reason to believe that numerous other people haven't done so too. My point is that if you accept the psychologist's verdict, that the only thing possible is to look for the trauma, for the pain, for the suffering, for the damage that COVID can cause you, you would lose perspective on those wonderful opportunities that it has provided you and numerous other people with too.

Jamie Now I am reflecting and wondering if I looked at the blessings with any of my own clients. I don't know if I did, and to some extent I probably got caught up in their anxiety, their trauma and difficulties.

Moshe Ideally you should be able to hear their pain, their suffering, their anxiety and distress, but at the same time if you are able to listen to it, you may be able to discover that there are untold benefits there for them, or that it is there, but they are not aware, or they are aware but not telling you. They might think the job of a psychologist is to only talk about the negative things in life and not the desires, the pleasures, the opportunities.

Jamie Why didn't you tell me this two years ago, Moshe?

Moshe Because I realised you could work it out for yourself.
Jamie But I didn't!
Moshe You know, a lot of people who have benefitted have kept quiet about it. It's difficult to enjoy your food if you are in the company of people who are starving.
Jamie Yes, I wrote that in my book too – that several times I didn't want to see people when I was so happy in lockdowns, but you were a safe person I could discuss it with.

*

Half an hour into the phone conversation I told Moshe I had another question for him but checked if he was tired and would prefer to stop.

'Ask,' he said.

*

Jamie You've already spoken about psychology, but what about all the psychologists? I have noticed several colleagues, myself and some friends, all quite burnt out at times. Many have families, kids at home, and the stress was huge. I know you joked at the start, saying that COVID was created by psychologists and business and money etc, but what about the human side? As psychologists we were finished, I was even a bit burnt out at the end of last year. We spoke about it, but what about managing the human side and never-ending waiting lists of children to help?

Moshe Look. Apart from being professional, psychologists too are members of society, and they are no different.

Like everyone, they are subject to all the pressures and opportunities. Now it may well be that to some it was an impossible life. I don't want to, for one minute, ignore the very painful challenges that COVID caused to an untold number of people. And some of them people with young children, or others, it was very very difficult for them. Having said so, if you work with a framework that does not allow you to see the opportunities, the only thing you are able to see, because that is the only tool your profession has given you, is to look at the dark side, then you will be in trouble yourself. As a person and as a professional. If it is always dark, you just bump into things, and you don't see anything. You need to see the light; you need to see the opportunity.

Jamie Can I tell you something quickly. Last night I watched the talk on humour in therapy and in life that you gave seven years ago, and it is the same message. You said there is light and darkness, there is light and heavy, and there is seriousness and humour and that makes a whole being. I literally watched it last night, Moshe! (We both giggled.)

Moshe You mean you are telling me I am boring. I am repeating myself.

Jamie No, no, don't be silly!

*

"There are always miracles in the world, even when it seems dark."
—Eddie Jaku, *The Happiest Man on Earth*

Moshe Let me take this in a totally different direction. I have probably worked more than just about anyone else, or very few people have worked with Holocaust survivors for as long as I have. I have not only worked with Holocaust survivors, but their families, their children and grandchildren too. Jamie, even with Holocaust survivors, one of the things they tell me is how, in the worst circumstances, their capacity to use humour helped them to survive the Holocaust. And to be functional after the Holocaust. And further, in the Holocaust, which was arguably the most traumatic event in human history, people have benefitted. By which I mean it has been the material for and the incentive of growth and development. Some great books were written as a result of the Holocaust. Music was written, humour was created, and I could go on and on.

I titled the book in which I describe my work with Holocaust survivors *Resilience*, because that has been an aspect of Holocaust survivors. But when you forget about the therapy and look at it sociologically – in Israel, after the war, half of the people who enrolled in medical school were Holocaust survivors. There are people who missed education, and nonetheless half of the intake to medical school were Holocaust survivors. In the Israeli army, the most difficult area of training, the most difficult area to get into is pilot training and again, about half of them were Holocaust survivors.

Jamie   Moshe did you do that?

Moshe   Number one, I wasn't a Holocaust survivor. I am a Palestinian. I was born in Palestine. I was in the tank unit and again there were Holocaust survivors serving with me in the army. I am saying that Holocaust survivors were able to get into the most difficult and demanding units, both in the army and at university.

To think that trauma is only damaging to you is damaging in itself. To look only at the positive also is terrible denial. Ideally you should be able to see the light and the dark.

*

"Suffering becomes a fearful gift, that cultivates character."
—David Brooks, *The Road to Character*

CHAPTER 19

Story Time

Moshe almost jumped out of his chair and his entire demeanour changed. I had imagined we would be wrapping up and preparing to end the session and he just started talking. His eyes were wide, he was passionate and enthusiastic. I was entirely immersed in the stories he shared, learnt a lot and was excited about creating the final chapter in my book. On that day, I didn't walk out of his office until 6.30.

*

Moshe I'll start by telling you now, after last week, when we talked and you recorded it, I kicked myself. I wanted to say more. I thought of various examples of people, the examples that are significant to me, of heroes in my life that have provided an example for me, of how crisis is an opportunity – the theme I was talking to you about. Jamie, there is nothing wrong with talking about the dangers, so long as you say there is also an opportunity here, and I want to share them with you.

Aharon Appelfeld is a man who was a Holocaust

survivor. During the war, he ran away with his father after he witnessed his mother being murdered by the Germans. They ran away, and at one point he got separated from his father as a kid. He survived by running around with a group of robbers, thieves and, at a different stage of life, he lived with a Ukrainian prostitute. Throughout all that time he realised, as a child, that if he spoke people would realise that he didn't come from there. His accent would betray him and he would get killed, so he pretended to be deaf and dumb. He did not speak. He survived the war without speaking, and at age fourteen he went to Israel and for the first time in his life, where he was in what we would call some normal environment, he said to himself out loud, "Who am I? What is my name? What do I know about myself?" He started by saying to himself, "My name is…", and he said it. "My mother's name was… My father's name was…". And he slowly and gradually recovered his memory. In the process he also taught himself Hebrew, and the way he taught himself Hebrew is he copied a chapter from the Bible every day.

At one point he wrote his first book about his memories. He sent it to a publisher, and other publishers, and they refused to publish it and said they were in a new country, busy building their country, and suggested he write about what was happening there rather than depressing things from the past, etc. Until two guys who knew him – I actually knew one of them too – published his book with their own money. He continued and eventually he published close to fifty books about his experiences.

To many people he is regarded as the great writer of the Holocaust. When he was told that he always rejected it and said, "I did not write about the Holocaust, I wrote about my life. I wrote about myself and my memories and in fact I did not write about the period of time of the Holocaust." He wrote about before and after the war, but it evokes the Holocaust.

The point really is, from my point of view – I don't think the Holocaust was a good thing, no one would recommend it to anybody, but this man found a way to make the Holocaust the stimulus as well as the material of his literature. Lots of people expected him to win the Nobel Prize, which he did not, but arguably he deserved it. That is a powerful example, Jamie.

The other one I wrote about in my books is Shalom Heichem, in *Resilience*. What happened is he had a very abusive stepmother, who would abuse him and swear at him. His first publication was a glossary, a dictionary of all the swearing she did. It was a wonderful piece of writing, and he became one of the greatest Yiddish writers of all time. And not just that, he went to America, and in New York, the most heavily attended funeral of all time was that of Shalom Heichem.

Jamie I am going to re-read that chapter tonight.

*

In *Resilience* Moshe writes, 'I love the way he (Shalom Heichem) solved his stepmother's problem. A wonderful example of "don't get mad, get even", or "writing is the best form of revenge".' This is powerful evidence that pain and trauma can be a stimulus for creativity and growth.

*

Moshe Jamie, I have a whole collection of these stories because I was thinking about it after we spoke last week. In the Greek world, who was the greatest orator of all time? A man called Demosthenes. Why? Because he was a stutterer and a stammerer – he could not speak properly. And the way he cured himself, he would go and walk along by the sea with stones in his mouth and train himself to speak to overcome the waves and the stones and became the best orator of all time.

Jamie I don't even know what an orator really is.

Moshe In our profession it may be Milton Ericson, who was a medical hypnotist, but basically, he was a great therapist. There are a number of books written about him, one by a famous family therapist called Jay Haley and the other by Sidney Rosen, who wrote a book called, *My Voice Will Go with You*, which is what Milton Ericson would tell his patients. Milton Ericson himself suffered from polio, so he was handicapped. He would often say to his patients, 'You don't have my advantage, you don't suffer from polio.' It was a beautiful way of saying that there are advantages to disadvantages.

*

I had never seen Moshe talk so passionately.

*

Moshe And today as I was talking to my previous client, who you saw walk out, he didn't know it, but it reminded me of another wonderful example. There is an Australian writer, Barbara Blackman, who was married to an Australian painter, Charles Blackman.

Jamie I have heard of him, I think.

Moshe She was his ex-wife – they separated – and she was partially blind. He painted her very often. She wrote a book titled *Certain Chairs* in which she described beautifully how, by virtue of her blindness, the chairs meant more to her because she could feel them. She described how her blindness made her life richer. And now I have another story to tell you, which I didn't even think about before.

Jamie Moshe, this is just amazing. Please tell me!

Moshe At one stage, maybe I wrote it, maybe not, I played tennis and got hit by a tennis ball. I did write it, in *Corrupting the Young*.

Jamie What was the advantage of that? I did read it, but I can't remember it right now.

Moshe They put me in bed, blinded, for a week and I titled the story "A Privileged Man", I remember now.

Because the doctor said I had to stay in bed with my eyes covered but gave me toilet privileges – I was allowed to go to the toilet, so I played with that. In the book, it is written, like this: "I was a lucky man who no longer had to feel guilty, because now I had been granted toilet privileges". After a week of lying in bed, I was allowed to get up. For the first time, I was sitting at the kitchen table and Tesse served me lunch. And after lunch, I took my plate and I walked to the sink, washed the plate, took a rag and wiped the table. The truth of it is the experience of wiping the table was one of the most exciting experiences in my life. I did not write about that because I thought it was too wanky, too new age.

Jamie I understand what you are saying fully.

Moshe The truth is, that was a simple truth. I enjoyed it after a week of that deprivation. The physical experience of wiping the table was great. I've just connected it to Barbara Blackman, who was also blind, but she was blind for life and I experienced what she was writing about.

Jamie Because for that week you couldn't see?

Moshe Yes, because for that week I was blind.

Jamie Moshe, now I have another chapter. All these stories that you have shared today aren't linked to COVID, but they are all linked to hope.

Moshe They are all linked to the fact that crisis is opportunity, that no matter how bad things are, you can turn them into advantages, that emptiness can have untold possibilities.

Jamie   Can I link it to one more thing? It's the theme of my book – look what my story has given me. If I didn't have all these difficulties, I probably wouldn't have met you. There is always the other side. There is the sad and the hard side, but there is the good side too. Thank you, it has been amazing, and by the way, Moshe, I have plagiarised you.

Moshe   For this I have a quote from T.S. Eliot, who said, "Immature poets imitate, mature poets steal", so be mature and steal from me with my blessing!

*

"Hope is a function of struggle – we develop hope not during the easy or comfortable times but through adversity and discomfort."
—Brené Brown, *Atlas of the Heart*

CHAPTER 20
Baptism by Fire

One morning I was lying in my bed, half-awake, looking forward to a slow morning where I could walk through the gardens to my coffee shop, make a yum breakfast, curl my hair and get to the office by 11 am. I'd had an emotionally hard day before and needed a nice morning. At 8.30 my phone started ringing and I saw it was a mentor who shared there had been a fire where I worked and I needed to get there as soon as I could. She explained it was important to cancel all clients I had booked in my office as this was an emergency and because of my familiarity, they would need to see my face there.

What a way to start the day! I was very confused and still half asleep. I ran out of my apartment within exactly seventeen minutes. I was terrified, did not want to go, did not know what to say or what to do. But just as with the Autism Spectrum talk the year before, I knew I needed to go and I knew I would probably be okay, even if I was slightly hysterical.

There are two things in my life that I am very scared of – snakes and fire. Last summer I was going with a friend to a beautiful rock pool which was a thirty-minute bush walk away from the car. It was a hot day, and I knew there would be snakes around, but I used my psychology skills on myself on the way there. I told myself, look, there might be snakes far out in the bush, but I won't see one. They are more scared of me than I am of them. Enjoy the walk and don't let this phobia stop you from enjoying your day. I also told my friend not to say the S word.

After the most magical day we decided it was home time and walked up the ten steps back to the path. My friend, who was in front of me, suddenly looked extremely startled and put her hand out for me to step back. There in the middle of the path was what I would call a huge (and my friend would call a smallish) grey and blue snake. I nearly died. I turned and sprinted back down the ten steps, hyperventilating. My friend, who was very scared, watched the snake crawl back into the bush, came down the stairs and pulled me straight back up. This was the closest in my life I have ever had to a panic attack and although it makes for a funny story, it was another one of my worst nightmares come true. A real Australian bush snake witnessed by Jamie who has a real snake phobia. Comparing seeing a bush snake or bumping into all my family friends on a date, I think the bush snake is worse, to put it into perspective. Much worse in fact!

My friend was amazing and knew if she didn't get me back on the bush path in that moment she never would. I agreed to go, but only if she held my hand *the entire time.*

'Jamie, it's thirty degrees! I am not holding your hand the entire walk back, but I am right here with you. I promise you we'll be okay.'

Talk about exposure therapy. Having to walk through the bush where the snake was for thirty whole minutes. Worse than the scariest movie ever created. I was hyperventilating for the entire walk back and my friend told me stories to distract me, which I couldn't even listen to. They went in one ear and out the other. She reminded me to breathe, as she would hear me hyperventilating and see my head moving from side to side in paranoia. When we got back to the car, I was shaky and of course we had a laugh. On the way home I made her stop at a 7/11 to buy some lollies and a coke. I was still so shaky. She told me it was so strange for her to see me like that, and that she'd never ever seen me such a mess before. I told her I hated the place; the rock pools weren't worth it, and I was never ever coming back. I also eventually told her that the experience would probably make me a better psychologist because now I could understand what it's like to have significant physiological fight/flight and adrenaline symptoms, something many people had described to me, but I'd never personally experienced before.

Now, I had to face my second fear. I had to go into a school which had just had a fire in a psychologist role and offer support to those who needed it. Of course, on the way there in the car I called my mum.

*

Jamie Hi Mum, good morning. Omg, school has had a fire, and I have to go in! They just called me. Have a look – I think it's on the news.

Mum What?

Jamie Mum, I don't want to go! You know how scared I am of fire. What do I even say to the people? How am I possibly meant to do this?

Mum Jamie, doll, you're the psychologist, not me. (She said, laughing.) Just go in there and be yourself. They love you there. You will know what to say, I promise. You'll be fine. Just think about the children and do it for the children.

Jamie I'm so scared, my heart is beating so fast. I don't want to do it! (I remember as I was driving, I thought my heart was literally going to pop out of my chest I was so scared.)

Mum I promise you will be fine, my baby. They need you and you can do this. (I started to get closer to the school and panic even more.)

Jamie Mum, I can't even think clearly. I don't think anyone is hurt. But I'm not even being funny, can you please tell me what to say to them? I've never been in such a situation before. What can I possibly say?

Mum Look, it's not a tragedy because no one was hurt. Remember I always told you when you were travelling that as long as you were okay there was nothing else that mattered. Tell them that it is just a building, and it will be okay. It is very lucky that none of the little children were in there. As long as everyone is okay, it doesn't matter.

Jamie OMG Mum, I'm driving in now. I am so, so scared. I can't do this.

Mum   Of course you can. You will be fine, my darling. Call me if you need me and good luck.

Jamie   Bye Mum.

*

And then my own baptism by fire occurred. Whereby the big baby who is terrified of fires hung up the phone, pulled herself together, marched into the school and, dare I say it, did a pretty good job. It was a very interesting and strange day. I don't think anyone knew how they were 'supposed' to be feeling. Everyone was in shock and running on adrenaline, including myself. For some reason, I remembered a two-day course in Psychological First Aid I did in my first week of masters. It was terribly boring, but the main message I recalled was to be there with the people in the moment, and not to worry about the future. And that's what I tried to do. I ended up talking to different people throughout the day, trying to do the best I could.

'I am just so shocked,' one teacher told me, holding back tears.

'Of course you are. I am too,' I said.

The part that stood out to me was the way in which the school staff and community beautifully came together in such a difficult and turbulent time.

The following day I went back to the school very early and it was harder than the previous day for everyone. Again, I roamed around the school, trying to be useful and mainly listening to staff and students share their feelings and experiences. I don't think I had too much to say to anyone, I don't really know what one *could* say in such a situation. But what I have come to realise is that having the space to talk about what was going on was helpful for everyone involved. It was a hard balance for me, trying to show staff I was there if they needed support, but not being annoying to them. I do worry that I might have been annoying, but I think that is just my mind making up stories, as many said how appreciative they were of my support.

Children are incredibly resilient and the blessing in this case was that it happened before school when no one was there. I think that is the luckiest thing possible. While I was doing this support work, I kept thinking of my book and the themes in it, trying to look for the light in this darkness. I said such things as 'We have a lot to be grateful for. It's very lucky there weren't any children in the building at the time.' 'Look how your community has come together in such a time of turbulence. It is something to be very proud of. It was so beautiful to watch.' 'Imagine the new Kinder you will be able to design one day. It may even be better than the one that is gone.'

I slept at my family home that night as I was so exhausted after dinner I didn't feel as if I could drive home. I woke up feeling weak and vulnerable. My mind was okay though – my heart was not hurting about the fire and in fact I have been much sadder and more traumatised by workdays before. I was not sick either, my body had held it together, but I felt shaken up and extremely fragile. My good friend had texted me the day before, inviting me to a yin yoga retreat which would be the most perfect outlet for me. I went and it felt so good to stretch my body, as I was quite tense. Finally, when the end of the class came – the Savasana – the teacher put on a meditation, the entire meditation was about fire and something burning down to nothing with black ashes everywhere! I kept thinking to myself, No, surely not, I am imagining it, and then I would hear the words 'fire and ashes' and I could not stop laughing. I don't know what the message in this was or why the meditation had to be linked to fire that day – it was so strange!

I had a bubble bath and read more of Brené Brown's book, *Atlas of the Heart*. I was up to Part 6, 'The Places We Go to When We're Hurting (anguish, hopelessness, despair, sadness and grief)' and thought it would be fitting and definitely useful for the position I found myself in. Brené wrote about hope, hopelessness and despair, and I learnt so much from it – for myself, for my book and for the school that had just faced a traumatic event.

Brené writes how hope is a cognitive process and a 'way of thinking'. I never knew that. Hope comes from setting realistic goals, figuring out how to achieve those goals and having agency and belief that they can be achieved. I really loved this concept and reflected how that is exactly what had occurred at school the previous week. The leadership team had quickly made a plan for moving forward which instilled hope – in the staff, in the children and the community – that things would be okay, and they were!

For me, the following two weeks were perhaps the most challenging I have ever faced as a psychologist. My lady-of-leisure life was taken away from me and in the first week I woke up at about 7 am three out of five days. I don't think I have done that since I was at school myself! I spent most of the time I wasn't in the clinic at the school, which resulted in very long days.

*

Jamie   Mum, I don't even understand how people work from 9 to 6. it's just so hard I don't get it.
Mum   No, Jamie, your work is different. You are giving all day and talking to people. It's different from sitting at a computer.
Jamie   I don't know, Mum, but it's not for me.

*

The thing I was most scared about after facing the school that morning was my body crumbling on me. My mind was strong enough to manage the work, in fact I enjoyed most of my days, but the pattern with me is that my body is not as strong as my head. I had to practise what I preach and take care of myself, and somehow, I did. Although I was exhausted, I was managing well, which surprised me no end.

The following Wednesday I had been at the school from 7.45 am – 4 pm and had my 5 pm appointment with Moshe. I was exhausted, to say the least. I kind of wanted to cancel as I didn't know how I would possibly have any words left, but more than that I was looking forward to debriefing with him about the week I was experiencing.

*

Jamie   Hi Moshe. You don't even understand what's happened to me this week. (I told him a day-by-day account of the previous six days.) I am sorry I am rambling so much to you. I don't know why I

	am telling you what happened each day. It probably doesn't even matter.
Moshe	First of all, you are not rambling, and maybe it is useful for you to put it into perspective by telling me what has occurred.
Jamie	Yes, it really is. I'm not sure why. Moshe, let me also tell you it is a miracle I haven't got sick. I do not know how, but I am so happy my body has handled this.
Moshe	It is interesting you mention being sick. As soon as you walked in the door, I thought to myself that you were looking very healthy and good today.
Jamie	Yes, it's so weird – a few people have told me that, but I don't know how.
Moshe	Well, Jamie, maybe you have learnt that in fact as a psychologist you are much more able and competent in doing something you never thought you could do. And it sounds like you have done a good job. Sometimes it is only in these situations we learn our true capabilities, and it can be a very rewarding feeling.
Jamie	Oh my goodness, if you had asked me if I could have done this I would have said definitely not. I wouldn't even have questioned it. But the weird thing is, despite the long days I am even enjoying myself somehow. Is that weird?
Moshe	No, it's not weird. It's a good learning for you. It's a trial by fire, I think the saying is.
Jamie	What is that?

Moshe Look it up. Maybe it can be another chapter in your book. The 'saviour' who comes into school as a psychologist to help the people in the traumatic situation, but really on the way there she was on the phone to her mummy, very scared and asking her what to say.

*

And we laughed together.

*

Jamie Yes, Moshe, that is such a good idea and it's so funny because it is just so true. That's exactly what happened!

CHAPTER 21

My Intention

I started writing this book on a Friday afternoon, and for some reason on the following Sunday morning I messaged three boys, saying, 'Hey, I'm writing a book and you're in it.' None of them seemed to respond too quickly and I was quite surprised. While I am a prankster and cheeky and love to play jokes on people, I really just wanted to let them know about the book.

I ended up speaking to one of them on the phone about it and he asked me what I was writing and why. When I explained it to him, he said it sounded interesting and asked me what my intention was for writing the book. It really made me think, because I had no idea what my intention was, who the book would be aimed at or why I was even doing it. But as I have been writing, my intentions have become clear to me.

The following week I proudly printed a copy of what I had written so far to give to my grandparents to read, as I thought they would love it. When I spoke to my Bobba the next day on the phone, she told me how sad it made her feel and that she cried the entire way through. I was genuinely shocked. 'It's funny, not sad! It makes me feel so good writing about it all.'

Bobba answered, 'I loved reading it, you write beautifully, but I just wish I wasn't reading about my own granddaughter.'

She explained to me how much she loved me, and how amazing I was and that I would settle down at the right time. I told her that what I have written may have been too confronting for her, but it was nothing she didn't already know. Once again, my intention in writing this book was definitely not to make my Bobba cry and feel sorry or sad for me. She also wanted to kill me when I told her I had added this paragraph into my book and said to my Zaida, 'Can you believe her? I can't say anything in front of her now. Everything I say will just go in the book!' And the three of us sat laughing together.

With my original idea of writing a book with Moshe, I thought how honourable it would be for me, but instead, I've realised that part of this book has been to honour him and the beautiful work he has done with me and others. He has contributed considerably to the field of psychology, not just in Melbourne but around the word. He has taught and supervised several young psychologists, written standardised tests, books and clinical papers and worked individually with hundreds, if not thousands, of clients and families. He is wise. He is humble. He is so extremely kind. I feel as if a star was shining on me the day he called to say he had a cancellation and that he was willing to see me.

In June 2013, Kim Beiber, a psychologist who also worked at Williams Road Psychotherapy Centre, interviewed Moshe after he had reached the milestone of fifty years in practice, titled 'The Joy of Therapy'. At the time Moshe had worked in his room for thirty-four years, and now it has been forty-three years. I watched the six-part video of that interview a few years ago and recently found it again on Moshe's website. I was blown away by so many of the things he said that I had written about throughout this book.

My personal journey with Moshe, my experience as a therapist in therapy, has made me believe in the profession of psychology even more. It is truly a special field, not only to work in but to take part in as a human being. Part of my intention in writing my story and including our verbatim conversations about the most private aspects of my life was to show the readers that it isn't always scary. Yes, it is confronting, yes it hurts, yes, it is annoying and uncomfortable at times, but the rewards far outweigh the discomfort, at least in my case they have. In today's world mental health is much more widely accepted and there is much less stigma attached to seeing a psychologist than there used to be. But still to some it is confronting and a difficult concept to comprehend. In this book, I have tried to show how fun it is, how you can cry and laugh at the same time, and how worthwhile it can be when you find the right therapist that works for you. I know it's definitely not always easy.

In Moshe's book, *Corrupting the Young*, he describes how he asked a family he had worked with to send him feedback about what they remembered of the family therapy eight years later. Something in the father's response stood out to me: 'I think if people know you visit a psychiatrist, they think you are a nut, but they are very uneducated people – if they knew what a help it is, they would change their minds. I would recommend it to everyone.' And, Mr Peters, I would too.

In my story I have also tried to share how difficult it can be as a new and inexperienced psychologist. While I have been very lucky to work with the best psychologists and support team, it has taken me several years to feel vaguely comfortable in what I am doing. And, as Moshe explained to me, that is okay, that my anxiety about this showed that I was responsible and that I cared. So, in writing this book I have tried to show other young psychologists that it is okay to be scared at the start, and it is normal to feel anxious. The work can be draining, ever-changing and challenging. Not one day is the same as the day before, and not one hour or one session is the same as the one before. You plan and prepare for one thing, and never know what is going to come up. And you don't necessarily have time to think it through, when the surprises do come up and you are sitting opposite your client. You have to think on your feet and need to be flexible.

In Moshe's interview 'The Joy of Therapy', Kim Bieber asked him what advice to give to young psychologists:

*

Kim   What's important about therapy? What would you say to people who are beginning their career? Are there particular things you would want people to hear about when starting their journey?

Moshe As a teacher of therapy, and I try to practise it myself, I believe in it deeply – sooner or later you have to be your own person, you can't be somebody else. To really be effective, you need to be yourself. To me, I didn't want to be a teacher where my students would follow in my footsteps. I regard that as a failure in a teacher. Success is that they find their own way, and I somehow played a part in them finding their own way.

To be committed to one way of working and not be influenced by other ways of thinking and working is inconceivable. Ideally you acquire and understand a number of ways of working and you find your own way within it. If you want to talk to different people you need to understand different languages. Ideally you need to be able to work and think in a number of different ways.

I usually don't tell people to study psychology – it's as boring as hell. The study of psychology is boring, psychologists are boring, and most people don't listen to me. I am comfortable with people not listening to me. For me, the study of psychology was boring but the working as a therapist has been deeply rewarding.

*

Moshe then discussed his yoga and meditation practice and mentioned how 'in that self-care sort of a way we look after ourselves' and how that impacts how we are as therapists.

For me, psychology is a very rewarding occupation. It

is a true privilege to sit and have people share their most intimate thoughts, feelings, and stories with me. Since I began, I knew it was right for me, and I am spending each day doing what I love.

*

In the Joy of Therapy interview, when Moshe was asked about being a psychologist for fifty years, he said:

Moshe I enjoy it, I enjoy it greatly. Enjoy is too superficial a word. I find it deeply, deeply satisfying. I find it challenging, exceedingly interesting. Positive psychology discussed the concept of flow – of being totally absorbed in what you are doing. I have never felt bored, really never. And in fact, when I do feel bored, I find it very interesting in dealing with my boredom. I feel very engaged and very involved in the work itself. The other thing is that the work is meaningful, and it is very meaningful for me. It is engrossing because I find it deeply satisfying at a simple human level. I feel the connection with the other people I work with – the connectedness is a deep source of satisfaction for me. I find it intellectually terribly absorbing, and I feel the strongest feeling is the feeling of being privileged, people trusting me and sharing with me their life stories.

When I was a beginning therapist I was concerned to do it right, that people would notice that I didn't know, that I would reveal my ignorance or do harm. By and large it is not an issue for me now. It is not an issue because I am very comfortable about telling my clients that I don't know something. I am very comfortable saying I don't know or I want to think about it. Or when I am worried about harming them, I tell them that that may not be helpful. It is a very liberating thing. I see a number of people who are in the profession and many of them formally know much more than I do, and I don't mind. If you are comfortable in your relative confusion and uncertainty, then I think you become a better therapist – but it is not so easy to do that when you are a beginning therapist.

*

At a later stage in that interview, Moshe elaborated on the concept of flow. He explained that it is when you go into a completely different space, an altered state of consciousness, yet 'There is an inner contradiction because I always end on time. I start and end on time always.' I noticed that myself, that in my sessions with Moshe we would be booking the next appointment at 5.50 pm on the dot, and I would thank him and leave the room. This has made me feel better about finishing on time too, as I truly feel like I need the ten-minute break in between clients. My mind still harps on at me though: If you were a good psychologist, you would go over time. You don't care about your clients as much as other psychologists do who go over time. One interesting exception is that in my sessions 44 and 45 with Moshe I was leaving his room at 5.55 or 5.56, not 5.50 on the dot! I think writing a book added another layer to our therapy, and another topic that Moshe was happy and generous enough to spend a few more minutes discussing.

> *"You can be a drop of water, a stream, or the raging river, it doesn't matter which, as long as you're in the flow – because they are all moving toward the ocean."*
> —Buddha

Moshe said more about this in a later session, without knowing I had written about it. He explained that it is about learning to live within life's limitations.

'If I accept that I will give you fifty minutes of my time, I have to train myself to act in an appropriate manner which, in the end allows you to organise yourself and be disciplined and make good use of the time. It has numerous important life lessons and benefits. As well as the example I am telling you, I also need to take care of myself. I am working on the hour, so I start on time, and I need to go to the toilet, and drink and recover from one session to another, etc. The last thing I have to say about it is my joke. You know what psychologists say – if you are early, you are anxious, if you are late, you're hostile or resistant, and if you are on time, you are obsessional. No matter what you do in life, if you deal with certain people, you are wrong.

I am more moved and touched by my work than I ever was. Maybe I am becoming a sentimental old man. As a young therapist I was more concerned and anxious about my competency and worried about whether people would see how much I didn't know. Now a lot of the work isn't difficult for me in that sense. I do a lot without thinking and it just comes naturally. I can now be more with the person, sit with them in their joy or sadness. I am more moved now than I have ever been before.

My wife died two years ago. I took some time off. When I came back to work, I realised in retrospect I would have not continued to work if I had come back to work when I was too absorbed in my own grief and not able to listen. I realised no matter my own grief, for that fifty minute I was somehow able to be exclusively with whoever I was with. That is the deepest thing. I think I am never bored, and it is rare that I think of anything else apart from sitting with the people I am with. Listening, experiencing the feelings, thoughts and the energy. I feel deeply rewarded.'

While I am by no means comparing the situations, this part of Moshe's video reminded me of the moment I realised I was born to be a psychologist. It was in the final year of my degree when I was completing a placement at an organisation which helps people facing homelessness. I volunteered there on Thursdays and Fridays and loved it so much that I often thought at the time I should have been a social worker rather than a psychologist.

I had been working with a client who was occasionally unreliable. He saw me at 3 pm on a Friday and when he didn't arrive, I would go home early. On one Friday I was feeling very tired, hungry and simply 'not in the mood' to be there. I was secretly hoping he would cancel and I would go home early. I already had a few cancellations that day so called at 1 pm to doublecheck he was coming in. And of course, he was. I didn't know how I would get through the session and be able to be present with him. And then he came in, we sat down and before I knew it the fifty minutes was up. Not once did I think about how hungry or tired I was, or how much I hadn't wanted to be there, and after the session I felt much better than I had earlier in the day.

Wow, I thought, I have found my calling!

*

Kim also asked Moshe, 'How long will you go on for?'

Moshe When it is difficult for me to go up and down the stairs I might stop. I don't know. I do know when I go on holiday one day and don't want to go back to work. So long as I feel that I enjoy it, or maybe somebody will have to tell me I have lost it and don't have what it takes. So long as I am able to do it, and think I am doing it reasonably well, I will continue.

*

At the end of my first year working with Moshe I was terrified that he would retire at the end of the year.

*

Jamie Moshe, I'm so scared – are you still going to work next year?

*

And he told me that he didn't intend to stop working anytime soon. I immediately felt relieved and nine years after Moshe's Joy in Therapy interview, I can confidently say that he still has what it takes and he better keep enjoying it, because I am by no means ready for my therapy to end! I laugh to myself about how it has taken almost fifty hours for me to be even vaguely prepared to enter an *adult* relationship, and how many hours I will need when I am actually in one!

*

Moshe Something that has helped me last so long is the sense of autonomy. People enjoy their work when they control their work. I am more comfortable with the word autonomy. Since 1979 I have been autonomous. The autonomy to see who you want, to work the way you want, to take holidays when you want, etc, etc, to have that say, is one of the very significant factors in making me enjoy my work.

*

The autonomy I have in my work is exactly why my friends tease me about never being at work – but the way Moshe put it in this interview is perfect and it is part of the reason I believe I left the school to work in private practice. I will copy Moshe and say that for me, too, it is one of the reasons why I love my work and my life so much. I can choose what, where and when I want to work and when I want to go away, and make it fit in with my life. We are very lucky to have the flexibility we do in private practice, and I have embraced this most in the last three months.

*

Moshe When I think more seriously about my work, the longer I do it, you realise very often what you could say that is profoundly meaningful is very, very simple. You don't need to say much.

*

My healer once told me that I had become a children's psychologist because I had faced a significant difficulty in my childhood and my life journey is to pass on the help to other children in need. One part of writing this book is to support or show other people in my position that it can be hard when your family splits up. It can be hard when you are in your late twenties and find dating terrifying, when it is expected that it is all you should be focussed on. To some people, it is 'very hard being single' at my age.

I don't yet have the answer to this, and I am most definitely not an expert on dating or relationships. But I think it is important to enjoy life and have fun while finding your path. It doesn't need to be so serious. Dating and finding the *one* doesn't have to take over your life. There are lots of parts to life and whether you are single or not, it is important to make each day count, since tomorrow is not promised to anyone.

> *"Time is all you have, and you might find one day you have less time than you think."*
> —Randy Pausch, *The Last Lecture*

CHAPTER 22

Becoming More Myself

'I think I am finally growing up. It's taken me so long.'
'I don't think I would call it growing up. I think you are becoming more yourself.'

Now, I think he is right.

I am single. I am not in a relationship. I'm nowhere near ready to end my therapy. Yet, I am very happy and very comfortable in my place in life. In the interview about COVID that I did with Moshe, we discussed attending therapy even when things are good. I said that I'd found that clients often feel reluctant to attend when things are going well, and they sometime cancelled their appointments.

*

Moshe From my point of view, even when things are going well they can always be better. There's always another way of looking at it. If you have a good working, therapeutic relationship to be able to share your successes as well, you can still benefit from it in an untold number of ways.

*

Towards the end of each year, I will try to write in my journal about how the year has gone. And if I am feeling very inspired, I will even try to write goals for the following year. SMART goals that are specific, measurable, achievable, realistic and timely. I think for the first twenty-eight years of my life, one goal was to lose five kilos. Every single year I want to lose five kilos, and mainly around my tummy. I have always had a roll there, even at my skinniest. I would describe this roll as the 'bane of my life', but for some unknown reason, from 2021 to 2022 my entire stance changed. Instead of trying to get rid of my silly roll, I decided I was going to love it. It is a part of me that doesn't really budge, and I am going to be me and be proud, *even* with the roll on my tummy. And it's kind of working for me. It might have even gone down a bit once I stopped caring about it!

Another strong quote from Moshe's talk was, 'Pick the battles you are going to win and not the battles that are going to defeat you.' I think the roll on my tummy has won, and I don't want to spend one more second being defeated by it. I'm laughing to myself as I write this as I don't think it was the type of example Moshe had in mind when sharing that advice.

A huge life transition I have experienced in my time with Moshe was moving out of my family home and into my own apartment. My fluffy, pink sanctuary that is my happy place. Moshe heard all about this story from the start when I was looking at places to buy, to the finish, about four weeks later, when I told him I won the apartment I had wanted at auction for the exact amount that I was willing to spend. It was very exciting and I remember Moshe saying something along the lines of 'Jamie, I am so happy to have been part of this process with you. I have counselled many people, but I don't think I have ever helped anyone buy an apartment.'

I thought to myself at the time, That's strange. I don't think you actually helped me buy my apartment. If it was now, I would probably have said that to him, but at the time I just smiled and agreed with him.

Moving out of home was a huge part of me *becoming more myself*. I spent the first lockdown year preparing to move in, saving and buying the furniture I wanted, drawing out where things would go on the floor plan and running around picking up furniture pieces from people I found through Instagram. On the day I was moving, the mover asked me if I was an interior designer, another compliment I just loved and still do. My mum loves my place too and comes for sleepovers when we miss each other (we love them even if anyone else thinks it is very odd). I have made many wonderful memories there.

When I moved into my apartment, I was very unwell with a stomach condition, in which I couldn't keep food down. My diet consisted of Slurpees and snake lollies and my vitality on the Vega machine would have probably been ancient. My family and I had thought about cancelling the move and waiting for me to get better, but I was determined for it to happen on the set date. I remember sitting on a pink Moroccan poof I had bought while my eighty-year-old Bobba, my aunty and mum unpacked my kitchen and my house for me. My Bobba kept asking me 'Where do these plates go?' or 'Where do you want the mugs and glasses?' to which I told her, I didn't care. I didn't know how a kitchen worked. I'd tell her to just do what she thinks, Bobba definitely knew more than me about kitchens!

On that day, despite being unwell and lethargic, the only thing I cared about was unpacking my books and creating my rainbow bookshelf. I had planned it in my head for months, and it is one of the most special parts of my home. Built into the wall are six shelves from floor to ceiling. The first shelf is full of my black books, then white, then red and orange, then yellow, then green and blue and at the bottom pink and purple. All my books are related to fashion, psychology and life. I decorated the shelves in colour co-ordination with my sage, my crystals, Palo Santo, card decks, room sprays and incense. And now, my very own book.

While I have written about it, you can imagine the number of conversations Moshe and I have had about him reading or not reading my book. He has given me several hours of his time and told me I don't need to be so thankful and that he is deeply invested in this project and idea, but he still has not read it. Instead, he was very set on having conversations with me about it and not in my therapy time. I think the only date I've ever been excited about in my life was when I picked up Japanese dinner for the two of us and met Moshe at his office one night to review and discuss elements of this book I needed his input with.

*

Jamie   Moshe you know in the role of a serious psychologist of the APS, people might say this is inappropriate. Me coming here, talking about my book *out of therapy*. But, to me, it has helped me so much, legitimately changed my life to the point that I don't think another fifty hours of therapy could have. It is very out of the psychology square.

Moshe I agree with that. Look, there are many rules that are there to protect you, but we often don't think about what happens when those very rules stop freedom, spontaneity, growth and creativity. I understand the APS might not be happy with me.

Jamie This creativity has been the best thing you could have ever suggested to me, even if you are driving me mad by not looking at it.

Moshe Good therapy and good living is thinking creatively. And the more you engage me with your book, the more comfortable I am in encouraging you. You have your voice, and I don't want to spoil it. You are driving it – here is a metaphor.

*

Moshe proceeded to tell me a story about one of his favourite therapists, Milton Erickson, who told the following story about how he worked as a therapist.

*

Moshe Milton says that one day he was on a farm and his horse ran away. A day or two later, a farmer brought the horse back to him. Milton asked the farmer how he had found the way to his place. And he said, 'I didn't. I kept the horse on the road and the horse found the way.'

*

I think Moshe shared this anecdote with me because he believes it is the way he has worked with me throughout our therapy. Writing this book has been so much like attending my therapy. He has given me the support and strength from behind the scenes to be a big girl and write a book on my own, to believe in myself and my voice and to share it honestly. In the same way he has given me the support and strength through my hours of therapy to live and enjoy my life, be honest with myself and others around me, tell people what I really think and maybe one day even to be able to go on a date without having a nervous breakdown before.

Moshe has found the fact he has not read the book interesting too. He said to me, 'I have been thinking to myself about this process. Sometimes I think I should have respect for it and not interfere with it. Then I ask myself, Am I just being lazy? Then I give myself credit for restraining my own curiosity and think to myself, Trust Jamie, she won't make you into a fool. And on top of all of this, I am thinking to myself, Do I want to read it, and if so, when?'

There was a two-week period when I found my writing quite difficult and, to quote Moshe, I 'agonised' over it. He didn't think this was a bad thing, and in fact this time made me stronger, more determined and excited about my writing. When I went back to see him, I asked, 'Moshe have you lost faith in the book? To which he said, 'No,' in his serious teaching voice.

*

Jamie I think it might be time for you to read it now. Can you just read it, Moshe?'

Moshe No. I need to trust my gut and listen to what I think is right. In some ways I think I am giving you a compliment that is too big for you to receive. I have full faith in your book and your writing, and I trust you immensely, but I want you to keep going with it and not even care what I think. It really is a big compliment in a way.

Jamie Okay, fine thanks, Moshe. It's magical that I believe in it so much and I am so excited about it.

Moshe Have you shown the book to your dad?

Jamie I can't believe I didn't tell you! Of course I have. Let me read you the email he sent me. It was short, but it was one of the nicest and most meaningful things he has sent me.

Moshe Listen to what you have just told me. If I played a part in him telling you one of the nicest things ever, than who should care about publishing the book? This is a win in itself.

Jamie Dad wrote, "Jamie, I am speechless. Your writing is amazing and I am definitely going to have another read. You are an amazing daughter and writer. I couldn't be any prouder of you. Thank you for having the courage to share your story. Well done, my luv, and love you heaps, stay inspiring."

Moshe Now I will do what I have promised myself not to do and say put it into the book.

Jamie That's actually a good idea.

Moshe Your father has hurt you in the past, and you have spoken to me about your hurt, your disappointment and your pain, but on the other side of it he has arguably made you a better person. Really you are sharing with me success and resolution, and I am happy to hear it.

*

In growing up, in talking to Moshe, in leaving a job I had for several years, in moving into my apartment, and in constant lockdowns living through a pandemic, I have allowed myself to shape the adult life I want, the adult life I love. I am laughing to myself as I write this about how I am now referring to myself as an adult. In one of my own sessions last year, a teenage girl expressed to me that she found it 'hard to talk to adults'. I said, 'Oh, do you see me as an adult?' thinking obviously she wouldn't, and she stared at me with a confused face, and said, 'Yes,' as if it was the silliest question I could have asked. When I finished that session, I laughed myself and thought, Oh my G-d, am I really an adult? I don't feel like an adult. I can't believe she sees me as an adult.'

But maybe now I do.

For me, New Year's Eve has always been symbolic of how my year will go. I know this is completely made up in my mind, and not factual, but I feel that if I have a nice New Year's Eve, I will have a nice year, and if I have a weird New Year's Eve, I will have a weird year. And being a psychologist, I am the first to admit that, in my mind, I always find evidence to back up this thought.

On the most recent New Year's Eve, I went to my dear friend's house with a new friend I had made just as I was recovering from COVID. I wasn't particularly keen about going for some reason, and once again it turned out to be the most fun and magical night. The group of friends I was with are actually *old* now and many have babies, so they rushed home soon after midnight. There were about six or seven of us left and we started to play The Confessions Game from *School of Life*. One question asked in the game was, 'If you could have anyone's life but your own, whose would it be and why? I knew my answer immediately and was so excited and proud to share it in my drunk, high-pitched voice: 'No one's, I absolutely love my life and wouldn't want to change anything about it. I literally can't think of one other person's life I would want.'

Fast forward 6 months...

*

Jamie I would say I've fallen from heaven to hell in the last few months, and it is freaky to think about, Moshe. I have been tumbling, like down a rollercoaster, and I don't know where it's came from.

Moshe Well you know, Jamie, the higher you rise the further there is to fall. And that's what you've experienced.

*

My thirtieth birthday could only be described as wonderful. I had a fairy, gin and unicorn party with everyone I loved. It felt perfect to me. I remember looking at everyone singing me happy birthday and feeling so much love. And so much gratitude. And the next morning, I woke up, flew to Bali and began my yoga teacher training for 21 days. I would never have had the confidence to do this training had I not spent the previous months writing my book.

I remember arriving at the Yoga Barn on the first day of our training thinking, *wow what an incredible way to begin this decade, Jamie, you are so lucky.* And it was. I realised that the next three weeks was the first time I had not opened my laptop for an extended period in years. And it was also the first time I had not thought about anyone but myself in years. It truly felt so good and liberating, although I was tested beyond my imagination in the training. I was so far out of my comfort zone I was an anxious, sweaty mess. But, by the end of the 200 hours I had opened my body, opened my mind and my soul. I had a lot to integrate and take in.

I had previously put all yoga teachers on a pedestal and thought they were incredibly calm, zen individuals whom I deeply admired. Well, after my training, I decided if I was ever to write a book about it, the title would be, *Yoga is for Psychopaths* – myself included of course!

I came home from Bali the most tanned I have ever been. And while I had been shaken up in the training, I was in the best place I had ever been in mentally. Maybe too confident? Arrogant? Or maybe I finally saw the Jamie in myself that everyone else has always seen in me. I was excited to come back and step into my life with my newfound learnings. I was excited to stay calm and use my new tools while returning to a job I loved and home that is my safe sanctuary. I felt amazing in my body and in myself, as if nothing could get me down.

And then it changed.

It started with four bites in a line on my body, which freaked me out to an abnormal extent. I couldn't stop thinking about the bites and they did not go away. They were so itchy at night that my sleep became a mess and at the same time my anxiety levels rapidly increased. I was no longer this confident, young author, psychologist, yoga teacher but rather an anxious wreck. And an itchy wreck. The bites seemed unusual, and my upper thighs became covered in bruises from scratching so much, so I went to my GP who referred me to a dermatologist. The dermatologist told me to put steroid cream on the bites and take antihistamines, and that I would be fine. Well, I was most certainly not fine. I went back and was told to double the antihistamines and to keep cool at night. And that was it.

The itchiness worsened, my sleep worsened and so did my quality of life. I became scared of night time. Scared of my bed. Scared of the apartment that I had loved so much. Scared of being a psychologist. Scared of being single. Scared of going out and seeing my friends. And scared of being home alone. I was uncharacteristically unenthused by this book, and felt it was a lie, a fake. I was not enjoying my life, and in fact in those four months I wanted anyone's life but my own. I was constantly comparing myself to others. After getting so little information from any medical professionals, the only answer seemed to be that it was caused by stress and anxiety, which meant I needed to change my life around.

And on top of all the pain and mental anguish I was feeling, I couldn't even blame my dad for this one!

How could things be so bad? I would ask myself as I lay in bed. How have things spiralled so much? I felt like I was born to be a psychologist, but in this period, I would look at my calendar and feel anxious about every single client. How could I encourage others to help themselves when I was in such a rut?

I happened to have five very serious, complicated, difficult cases at that time and I resorted to mentors for supervision to get through. I tried to date in this time, too, and wondered if it was the anxiety that caused making me itchy. I was uncomfortable in my own skin and looking for anything outside of my body to calm me down. Of course, I didn't find anything. I went to yin yoga classes and left even more frustrated, as I would lie on my mat, trying to breathe, scratching my arms and legs. I eventually, accepted that I was going to be itchy for the rest of my life.

You don't know how difficult skin conditions can be until you are faced with them. I had never been particularly grateful for my non-itchy skin before that time and felt as if I should have been.

And then, on Christmas Eve, I received a phone call from a family member saying they thought I have scabies. Dreaded scabies, the old disease pirates got. They were right. For four months, I had mites living under my skin, literally ruining every part of my life, a life I had previously loved. It was so relieving to hear there was a medical reason behind my pain, and that it was so easily curable. Scabies is seen as embarrassing and not widely talked about, but I was anything but embarrassed to have found out what it was.

When I explained this story to Moshe, he asked if I felt anger towards the dermatologist who had missed it.

*

Moshe You know, Jamie, it sounds to me like it's medical negligence.

Jamie Yes, it absolutely is. But Moshe, how is anger going to help me? I haven't channelled my energy into being angry at all. I have just wanted to heal and build myself back up. How's it going to help me if I am angry? If anything, (I started to cry) I feel so sad for myself about how crazy I thought I was. Never mind anger, I am completely traumatised.

Moshe Well, as your psychologist, I want to tell you that maybe you should be angry. Sometimes a little bit of anger is a healthy response, and in this case it would be perfectly appropriate for you to be angry.

Jamie OK, I understand, but I'm still not angry. Did you notice in the last few months of sessions that I didn't even care about my book? I didn't even like discussing it with you because I thought it was so fake.

*

And then, his response, so relevant to all of us:

*

Moshe Well, Jamie, without your health your book means nothing. Without your health your work as a psychologist means nothing. In fact, there is an old Yiddish saying... *Abi Gezunt*... Without your health you are nothing.

Afterword

In Conversation with Moshe

Writing my account of therapy without Moshe reading it was a daunting task. I felt as if I had to be braver and more assertive than came naturally to me. I had to trust myself and my own judgement. So, when I had finished writing I decided to ask him about some its major themes and see if his answers matched mine.

Throughout this special interview Moshe seemed to be trying very hard to articulate something that comes intuitively to him, and he did a beautiful job of it. The part of the interview that stood out most to me was that the gist of his answers was simply about having always aimed to create an open space for me to talk about things. And that is what therapy comes down to, in a sense – the ability to be real and open and the benefit of simply saying things aloud.

I asked Moshe how he thought he/the therapeutic process had helped me in relation to my father, his answer surprised me. He said that it was something that I was still working on and probably would be for the rest of my life. When he answered this, for a second, I felt annoyed, thinking that after all my hard work in therapy and then my writing it would be 'fixed', and it seemed as though I was wrong. Here is our discussion:

*

Jamie How do you think you have helped me with my relation to my father and the relationship I have with him?

Moshe I'm not sure that I did. If I have helped you, it has only partly helped. Jamie, you see the process of you separating yourself from your parents, articulating who you are, who they are and how you relate to them is a life-long process. What I think has occurred through therapy is that we have created a relationship in which you feel free to tell me how you see and experience your father, and I have helped you talk through it and process it. We have created a social context in which you can explore and think out loud about your father. I think you have started to look at him in a more mature, objective manner. I might have asked you some questions to elicit more information but overall, there is a deep psychological process that will continue. I hope I have played a part in the healthy normal process of you growing up and seeing him more realistically rather than idealistically.

Jamie And what about my confidence? Do you think my therapy has helped me build my confidence in myself?

Moshe Yes, but your answer to that question is much more important than mine. You see, Jamie, I am holding a mirror up to you and asking you to answer your own question. Publishing a book about your therapy is confident and courageous. I have helped by listening to you, helping to point out the evidence of your ability, enabling you to talk about your misgivings and doubts. Exploring what you are scared of, when you are scared, what would the consequences be. That is how anybody helps. Part of one's confidence comes from good judgement and, Jamie, you are wise. At one point I was worried about your father getting upset about the book, but you have shown that you have enough wisdom to know what to say and what not to say. Jamie, it is real wisdom to know that, and if you have capacity for good judgement, you become more confident.

Jamie And what about me as a young psychologist? Do you feel you have helped me with my work?

Moshe I haven't tried to help you to be a better psychologist. I have tried to help you as Jamie. In fact, you as a psychologist has hardly come into the conversation, as I remember. To me the most important part is to enjoy your work. I enjoy my work. I am sitting here, as your psychologist and I am enjoying it. It is a challenge and I have spent a lot of time thinking about this interview, but I am happy to be here at 11 am on a Sunday morning. There is a sense of pleasure and joy in the creativity, but usually when I read about the way psychologists describe their profession and work it sounds like death, it is so mechanical and so little about real life itself. I think, directly or indirectly, I convey to you that I look forward to seeing you and take pleasure when you do well, and that is a different sort of psychology than the kind that is being taught at university.

Jamie And how do you think you have helped me with my fear of dating and relationships?

Moshe Jamie, with any anxiety the best way to help anyone is to encourage them to talk about their anxiety. Your anxiety about dating relates to the important man in your life and comes back to your father at one level. I think you are scared, because everyone of us gets scared of being rejected, and at a deeper level for you it is the fear of getting involved with someone like your father. It's genetic and biological – the relationship of a girl to the most important male in her life, whether it is her brother or father, would shape her experience of the opposite sex. So, talking about the dating you have done and about the most important men in your life is what we have done. There is a social influence that comes into play too – the way you see anybody in your life is not just about you and them but about the other people who have influenced the way you see things.

Jamie And how do you think my writing has helped me?

Moshe The job of any good therapist is to help people you work with to find their own ways to help themselves. In your case one of them is the writing. Writing is a way for people to calm themselves, to keep a record, to gain clarity, to make sense of their life and their world. Your difficulties in life have helped you to become a writer.

Jamie And finally, Moshe, have you noticed a change in me over our time in therapy?

Moshe: You are four or five years older, wiser. Resilient, you are more resilient. You have grown in an untold number of ways – in confidence, in your ability to reflect and articulate what you feel, in allowing yourself to dive into the deep end. Again, I will mention this: a 31-year-old psychologist writing an autobiographical study which includes her seeking therapy herself is evidence of courage. It is a very powerful example of courage.

REFERENCES

Blackman, B. (1998). *Certain chairs: Sketches drawn from our life.* Viking.

Brown, B. (2015). *Rising strong: The reckoning. The rumble. The revolution.* Vermilion.

Brown, B. (2021). *Atlas of the heart: Mapping meaningful connection and the language of human experience.* Vermilion.

Brooks, D. (2015). *The road to character.* Random House.

Dyer, W. W. (1976). *Your erroneous zones: Step-by-step advice for escaping the trap of negative thinking and taking control of your life.* Funk & Wagnalls.

Gottlieb, L. (2019). *Maybe you should talk to someone.* Scribe.

Haley, J. (1989). *The power tactics of Jesus Christ and other essays.* W. W. Norton & Company.

Harris, R. (2008). *The happiness trap: How to stop struggling and start living.* Exisle Publishing.

Harvey, S. (2020). *My year of living mindfully: How one woman found the power to transform her life.* Hachette.

Healy, J. (1989). *The power tactics of Jesus Christ.* W. W. Norton & Company.

Jaku, E. (2020). *The happiest man on Earth: The beautiful life of an Auschwitz survivor.* HarperCollins Publishers.

Jones, S. (2020). *My year of living mindfully.* Hachette.

Jung, C. G. (1969). *The collected works of C.G. Jung* (R. F. C. Hull, Trans.). Princeton University Press. (Original work published 1953).

Lang, M., & Lang, T. (1986). *Corrupting the young and other stories of a family therapist.* Renee Gordon Pty Ltd.

Lang, M., & McCallum, P. (2000). *The answer within: A family in therapy re-examined.* The Australian Council for Educational Research Ltd.

Lang, M., & Lang, T. (2007). *Resilience: Timeless stories of a family therapist* (Revised ed.). PsychOz Publications.

Pausch, R. (2008). *The last lecture.* Hachette Books.

Rosen, S. (1982). *My voice will go with you.* W. W. Norton & Company.

Sark, S. (1997). *Succulent wild woman.* Prentice Hall.

Watzlawick, P. (1976). *How real is real? Confusion, disinformation, communication.* Vintage Books.

INTERVIEW

Bieber, K. (2013). The joy of therapy: An interview with Moshe Lang. *Australian and New Zealand Journal of Family Therapy, 34*(3), 257–267.

WORKSHOP

Lang, M. (2015, May 7). Humour in therapy (A psychologist's humour is no laughing matter!) [Workshop presentation]. Australian Psychology Society (APS).

About the Author
JAMIE MASEROW

Photo Credit: Billy Toka @tokaphotography_

Jamie Maserow is a psychologist with experience in private practice and school settings, supporting individuals of all ages through a holistic approach to mental health and wellbeing. Passionate about the development of young people, Jamie uses therapeutic methods including Acceptance and Commitment Therapy, Cognitive Behavioural Therapy and Parent Training. She has a special interest in completing comprehensive psychological assessments, offering in-depth cognitive, social, and emotional evaluations to understand each child's unique profile and help them reach their full potential. Her knowledge spans neurodevelopmental disorders such as Autism Spectrum Disorder, Attention Deficit Hyperactivity Disorder and Specific Learning Disorders.

The Therapist in Therapy is her first book.

- the.therapist.in.therapy
- jamiemaserow.com

www.ingramcontent.com/pod-product-compliance
Lightning Source LLC
Chambersburg PA
CBHW060554080526
44585CB00013B/560